MW00810729

THE
GRAVEL
DRIVEWAY

Breaking the Cycle of Abuse

NANCY SLOAN

THE GRAVEL DRIVEWAY:
Breaking the Cycle of Abuse

Paperback: 978-1-952714-61-0
eBook: 978-1-952714-62-7
Editors: Flo Mayberry, Christine LePorte
Book Design: Shabbir Hussain Badshah

This is a work of creative non-fiction.
All of the events in this memoir are true to the
best of the author's memory. Some names and
identifying locations have been changed to
protect the privacy of certain parties.

Caution:
This book contains stories that some people
may find difficult to read regarding violence
against women and children.

Printed in The United States
by Ingram Content Group

Publisher
Mountain Page Press
Hendersonville, NC
www.MountainPagePress.com

MOUNTAIN
PAGE PRESS

CONTENTS

PROLOGUE

WHY WRITE ABOUT MY LIFE?

I t's 2021 and as I reflect on the forces that influenced my past decisions, I've attempted to piece together the fragments of my life in order to make sense of my choices. Now in my seventies, I've come a long way and I've thrived in spite of myself and others. The journey was rife with poor decisions, violence, sexual promiscuity, and betrayal; yet it was also sprinkled with joyful moments spent with family and friends, along with angels in the form of spiritual advisors that guided me to the answers I desperately needed to heal my wounded soul. Telling my story allows me to scrub the negative residue of my past and help my family and friends understand why I did what I did. I also want to encourage those in similar situations that there truly is a light at the end of the driveway.

I believe that prior to birth we choose our bodies and plan the experiences we must endure to reach enlightenment. Being enlightened is "becoming spiritually aware," and means that one has performed great service for humanity and will have a special place in heaven. Through adversity we build character, are stronger and more aware after we've been tested and have overcome obstacles. Each new experience teaches us different lessons and allows us to grow with every milestone until we reach that stage where we have completed our life's mission. I have reached many milestones and have a few more ahead of me on this journey.

It's important to tell my whole story so that I feel more fully understood and to bring hope to those in the midst of the struggle for freedom. I fought like hell over the years to take control of my life. As I embark on the task of writing this book I recognize the healing power of the endeavor and acknowledge my past along with the lessons I've learned from it. I look forward to the blessings yet to come. Like the mythological Phoenix I was reborn, but, unlike the Phoenix rising from the ashes, I did not emerge all at once from a blazing nest. Rather, I endured a slow burn that took many years, effort, and a desire to seek the truth before I rose up into hope and happiness. I've lived this story, the good and bad of it, and I alone can tell it.

CHAPTER 1
MY FAMILY:
OUR ROOTS

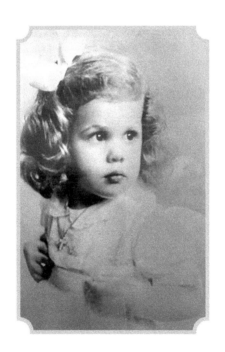

My story begins on January 22, 1947, in Brooklyn, New York, at Beth El Hospital where I was born into a family that included my parents, an older brother, Greg, and a sister, Maggie. I was the youngest sibling. I lived during some significant historical events in the world such as the beginning of the Cold War, the Roswell UFO incident, Israel attaining statehood, the separation of Pakistan and India into independent states, and the aftermath of World War II (1939 to 1945).

My father, Gasper Puglisi, was born in Sciacca, Sicily, in 1902, and immigrated to the US through Ellis Island, along with over twelve million other people. He first arrived with his family in 1905 but was not admitted because he was judged sickly by US immigration officials. Five family members—including his mother and some of his siblings—were allowed to stay in the US, but my father, along with several other family members, were sent back to Italy. He was cast off to bear the next years—a toddler without his mother. He returned nine years later in 1914, was admitted, and became a naturalized citizen in 1924. Those in-between years back in Italy without his mother had to be painful, although he never discussed it. I think it would have had a lifelong impact on him.

My father made the gym his focus, mostly boxing and bodybuilding, and he continued the practice regularly until he was in his eighties. It was a way of life for him and kept him healthy as he aged. He was a hairdresser and worked in one of the leading Fifth Avenue salons. This brought him into contact with people from high society, stage, and screen. I remember how glamorous the salon looked and going to some of the crazy fantasy shows that the Hairdresser's Board hosted.

The Puglisi's were a large Italian family, so of course we had extravagant meals on Sundays at my Uncle Tony and Aunt Mary's house. They were boisterous gatherings that included everyone with most of the family speaking Italian and gesturing grandly. My father helped prepare these meals and it was he that instilled in me my love of cooking.

My father was a loving, kind, and sociable man. In the Italian tradition, he kissed everyone, even men, on the lips. He had many friends and loved his family above all else. He knew my beliefs in the hereafter and supported them although he wasn't sure if any of it was true. He told me he would come back and visit me after he passed—and he kept his promise! He was the first love of my life and I will never forget him. He adored me and told me frequently. He called me "baby."

For me and my kids he was the "candy man." When I was a child he would take me to the 7-Eleven where I would fill up a bag with penny candies. It was a highlight for me and a sweet tradition he carried on with my children.

My mother, Anna Louisa deLaisne, was born in New York on September 26, 1914. She went by her middle name, Louise. Her father, my grandfather, Alberto deLaisne, was born in the Panama Canal Zone on November 27, 1886, and died in Florida in 1956. Alberto had French and Spanish heritage and immigrated to this country in 1908 at the age of thirty-two from Cuba speaking no English; he eventually went on to become a wealthy and powerful man within his community.

My maternal grandmother, Mary Kerling, was born in Lichtenfels, Germany, on August 1, 1883, and immigrated to this country in 1906 when she was twenty-three years old. She married Alberto in 1910 when she was twenty-six years old.

My mother had two sisters and one brother. Mom was the second oldest. According to my mother, my grandfather was a little man of five feet two who gained wealth by producing coffee bags. He was also an incestuous man who would enter his daughters' rooms and molest them. The independent ones—including my mother—fared better, but the meek sister who slept in a separate bedroom bore the brunt of the molestation because she remained silent. This quiet sister, my Aunt Bea, grew up to be an executive secretary, never had a boyfriend or married, and proclaimed "I don't need a man!" True to her word, she remained financially independent her entire life and when she passed, had money left over.

Alberto became the editor of a weekly Spanish newspaper. They lived in New York for a while then moved to New Jersey. Eventually, they came back to New York and settled in Brooklyn. They lived in a beautiful brownstone in a nice section of Flatbush, Brooklyn, that belied the sadness and sexual abuse that existed within. This was in the 1930s around the time of the stock market crash of 1929 and the Great Depression that followed. In 1932 FDR was elected and created the New Deal, which brought hope back to the American people. Swing-music dance bands such as Benny Goodman's Orchestra were all the rage as it was a time for the country to "set aside its problems and dance."

My brother, Greg, six years older than me, and my sister, Maggie, three years older, comprised the rest of my immediate family. Greg and I got along okay, but weren't particularly close, while I never really had a close relationship with Maggie. As the years went by, those feelings only worsened.

CHAPTER 2

GROWING UP:
SO MANY SECRETS!

Recollections of my childhood are awash in darkness. Long ago I lost my memories, but much later on with the help of my spiritual advisors, I was able to retrieve them. For better or worse, I was able to recover the ones that cut the deepest starting with the horrible fact that my sister heaped abuse on me beginning in what should be a safe space for babies—my crib. I learned this fact during the early days of my healing journey, and it set the tone for accepting the abuse that happened later on.

Early on our family lived in a modest, one-bedroom apartment before we moved to an affluent neighborhood when I was in the second grade. In contrast to the apartment, it was a split-level house on a beautiful, tree-lined avenue. There was everything to love, but I never felt comfortable there. I felt like an outsider, especially during my teenage years. I was so shy that I struggled to approach people and make friends.

In high school, I finally made a lasting connection with a girl named Loretta. She lived on the rougher side of town. Something about the danger there appealed to me and I ran to it defiantly and with jubilation. I could be completely myself with Loretta, defiance and all, and my rebellious nature was born. I hung out with one set of well-to-do kids in my neighborhood and curated a whole different set in Loretta's. These friends never met and I enjoyed a complete lack of competition and girl melodrama, which I loathed.

Another experience I was able to access from the black box of my memory during my healing journey was during my high school years. The father of one of my friends molested me several times. I was too afraid and ashamed to do or say anything about it, even though I knew it was wrong. No one in those days turned in abusers. Odd as it sounds today, it wasn't something the American culture had yet embraced. Now finally, thousands of American women, and many men, have come out of the shadows to confess that they had been abused. My confession is the same. Back then I too was abused and afraid, so instead of speaking out, I kept it a secret all these years.

My parents never had a traditional marriage—it was platonic or so it seemed. They slept in separate bedrooms and were never visibly affectionate towards each other. This was out of character with my father who I've already stated showed affection to everyone. In my mother's bedroom were two single beds, one which she occupied and the other which I often took to sleeping in because my dad had his own bedroom.

Not only did my parents sleep in separate bedrooms for most of their marriage, but my dad took separate vacations to Florida, went on golfing jaunts, and appeared to have a life apart from ours. The years when I slept in the twin bed in my mother's room, I took on the role of her protector—from what, I was never sure. All I knew was she had nightmares and would wake up screaming every night. She would get out of bed and walk to the window, open it, and scream, "I know you're there, I see you. I see you hiding under the bed." It was a scream of pure terror. She was in so much fear that it was hard to calm her down. I associated her nightmares with her father's incestuous behavior and conjectured that she most likely married a man eleven years her senior to escape her father. She seemed to be reliving those memories when she was sleeping. I would have to take her away from the window and put her back to bed, reassure her, and tell her it was okay.

I remember being ten or eleven when Mom told me about her affair. My brother and sister also knew. She would take me to lunch with him; his name was John. I got to know him and liked him. He was a very nice man, but I adored my father so it was a painful secret to keep. On our first meeting I didn't know what to think, but I did understand it wasn't a normal situation. I didn't know enough to be angry or rude, so I just went along with it. My mother had assigned me the role of her confidante in this dance of deception and any misstep would have caused irreparable damage to two families—so I kept quiet for years—as did Maggie and Greg.

My mother wanted badly for John to leave his wife but he never had the courage to do so. She dabbled in witchcraft, and would make potions and do ceremonial rituals to make his wife go away. I would ride in the car with her as she followed John's wife. She was obsessed with her and wanted to know her every move.

In the end, he never left his wife and my mother died of colon cancer at the age of sixty-four. Their relationship endured for twenty-five years in secret. When my mother became comatose we called for John to come while my father was at the funeral home making the arrangements. When he entered the room she sat straight up in bed and they hugged for a while. We all cried watching this emotional scene and left them alone. Soon after he left she passed peacefully. I was holding her hand and caressing her face. No one ever knew if my father was aware of her affair. If he did know, it was a secret he took with him to the grave.

CHAPTER 3

FIRST MARRIAGE, 1964:
A COOL CAR WASN'T ENOUGH!

It was the sixties and the beginning of the Vietnam War. Bloody Sunday happened during a civil rights march from Selma, Alabama, to the state capitol in Montgomery. There was a lot of civil unrest during this period which led President Johnson to sign the Voting Rights Act, to prohibit racial discrimination in voting. *My Fair Lady* won the Oscar for best picture. Woodstock and the British Invasion occurred along with the JFK assassination and the first man to walk on the moon. The sixties was a period of social and political change.

I had just graduated high school early at seventeen. During my last three years I had a boyfriend, Stan, who lived a few blocks from me in Garden City. His mother and grandmother were very controlling women. Betty, his mother, and especially his grandmother, whom we referred to as the Queen Mother, ruled it all. Stan was three years older than me. He was very conservative, which was everything that I wasn't. Why I was attracted to him, I honestly don't know. Suffice it to say I was young and impressionable and he had a cool '56 Chevy that he raced and taught me how to drive at fourteen. It was

Stan that I credit with fostering my love of cars. He would build and rebuild his car engines, taking them apart piece by piece and cleaning them. I would help him and that's where I learned a lot about cars and engines. We went to the race track frequently and I loved it. In the end, a mutual love of cool cars wasn't enough to save our relationship.

After I graduated, I knew I wasn't prepared for college so I went to work as a file clerk on Wall Street. I was still going out with Stan at that time and it seems that the first time we had sex, I got pregnant. Why no birth control, you ask? I guess I was too young and not educated on the limited methods that were available at the time. That's the best answer I have.

Informing my parents was difficult but I had no choice. To their credit, they took it well. My mother took me to a back alley woman to try to abort the pregnancy. I was clueless as to what was going on but it was clear my mother had arranged the whole thing. The woman put a catheter into my cervix, saying that injecting air inside my uterus would abort the pregnancy. I was a child, age seventeen, with no understanding of what was going on and had no decision in the matter. The problem was taken out of my hands and put into my parents' hands and I went along with whatever they told me to do.

We had a family meeting, because the back alley procedure didn't work and the pregnancy was never aborted. It was decided for us that we would get married. There was no other option in 1964. Deep inside, I was glad that nothing happened to the pregnancy, but I was not allowed to express those feelings aloud. Looking back, I was assaulted by that back alley experience and my baby was having none of it.

So into a family of controlling women I found myself. I was still a lost child masquerading as an adult and no one knew this better than Stan's mother, Betty. She exploited my youth and dictated our lives and I allowed her to do so because I was still in adolescent mode and in the habit of obeying my elders without questioning. Stan, too, was controlling—like mother, like son. Circumstances had brought us together. I was not her pick to marry her son and she didn't hesitate to let me know by her words and actions that she was not happy.

We were married by the justice of the peace and lived in an apartment in Richmond Hill. I quit my job in the city and prepared to be a stay at home wife and mother—because that was what women did in 1964—although at seventeen I had no clue as to what that entailed. Stan didn't like the way I cleaned, so his mother would come over with cleaning bucket and supplies in both arms and clean—on her hands and knees—over what I had just done while giving me the evil eye as she walked from room to room with her cleaning tools. It was a humiliating experience.

Right before I was due to give birth I twisted my ankle, resulting in torn ligaments. The doctor put a cast on it because of all the weight I was carrying. He said it would heal better with the cast. So at nine months pregnant I now had a cast on my foot and lower leg. This meant I needed supervision and assistance, so into Stan's mother's house we moved until I gave birth. In spite of our differences, I have to admit she took good care of us even though she didn't think I was a suitable mate for her son. Living in a home with someone whom I knew was not fond of me and wanted to control me caused the rebellion in my head to grow, albeit silently

On June 8, 1965, George Howard Eckstein, III, was born, a Gemini. He was a beautiful, healthy baby. I was in love from the moment I looked into his face and couldn't believe that he was now my child. It was unconditional love. I was a child mother and he was my baby doll. My wonderful parents taught me unconditional love and it came naturally to me, but actual parenting was a mystery. The birth was a blur because at that time I was knocked out with drugs and didn't participate. Between being asleep and awake, I apparently had given birth. Of course I didn't breastfeed because I didn't know any better and no one encouraged me to do so. Back in the sixties formula was popular and breastfeeding was discouraged.

As if it wasn't enough that Stan's mother came to my house with pail and cleaning rags, I was TOLD by Stan and his mother, that MY child would be named after his father, and that they had already chosen his godparents. I wasn't able to pick even one godparent for my own child. I had no say in the matter, even though I was his mother. I hated the fact that I had no voice in naming my son. Stan's mother kept calling him The Third. So from that we took TT or Tee and that was his name from there on within the family. Once again, I allowed it all to happen. Again controlled, again quiet, again rebellious—and the rebellion in my mind and body continued to grow more broadly and deeply.

Having a child together was not sufficient to sustain our marriage and it quickly soured. The rebellion in my mind drove me to make a move to leave. When Tee was about six months old, I left Stan and moved into my parents' house. After a year of separation I flew to El Paso, Texas, and crossed the border into Juarez, Mexico, for a quick divorce. Our youth and the fact that I had no say in naming my son, along with Stan's mother's constant interference, were the contributing factors that ultimately led to our divorce. I was eighteen years old, my hair was platinum blond, and how ballsy was I to seek a Mexican divorce?! Looking back, I can't believe I did that by myself. But it laid the foundation that I could make hard choices again in my future.

Stan was devastated, and to this day I don't believe he ever got over it. It is something he has shared with me and my daughters. Stan's grief caused him to withdraw and he abandoned his son, rarely seeing him. I believed Tee's presence would bring back memories for him that he didn't want to deal with. Stan's mother was the opposite. She adored Tee, saw him regularly, and maintained a close relationship with him over the years.

Sometime later, after the grief seemed to soften, Stan and I got back together. We had talked about getting married again. We thought we should try to make it work. What was I thinking? I was still young and making poor decisions. Ultimately, I couldn't go through with it after giving it careful thought and broke it off.

I see my relationship with Stan as the means to bring Tee into this world. The back alley experience was meant to extinguish him, but Tee was strong and resisted the effort. In hindsight, I regret none of what I had to go through to bring him here, as it was all worth the love I have and the bond I share with my firstborn son.

With a failed marriage and a child to care for, I was a wounded sparrow trying to survive. I needed stability and a place where I could finally take a deep breath and exhale. Instead, what I encountered next was far more sinister than the domineering mother-in-law and the mama's boy I had left behind.

CHAPTER 4

THE "TUDOR HOUSE OF HORRORS" AND OUR ULTIMATE ESCAPE 1967–AUGUST 1977

H ave you ever heard the saying, "Satan often comes cloaked in beauty or disguised in sheep's clothing?" Well, I had heard it but failed to heed the warning. I was rebounding from a failed marriage and had been divorced for about a year when I crossed paths with a classic wolf in sheep's clothing—in a bar! Being young and naïve, I failed to recognize the signs and was instantly smitten. Dan was not someone I would have previously been attracted to; yet upon our first meeting, his swagger, deep-set eyes, and confident demeanor were enticing and I fell immediately. We hooked up and I repeated the mistake of my first marriage. Once again I got pregnant and we chose to get married. I was twenty years old with a two-year-old son.

Two weeks into our marriage Dan was already cheating on me with other women and I realized that I had unwittingly plunged into marital life with a philandering husband bent on violent outbursts and temper tantrums which he directed toward me and my son. He would slap, punch, kick, and choke Tee to discipline him. I would put myself in between them so that Dan would hit me instead. Finally, I sent Tee to my parents' house to live with them—he was safe there. He wound up living with them for two years.

Dan went out most nights womanizing and came home drunk. I was never allowed to ask questions about his whereabouts or I would get slapped, punched, kicked, or have something thrown at me. This occurred from the very minute we were married. He brought me home a gift of genital warts from his adulterous behavior, and I was not allowed to question how I got it. We were married for ten years, and during this time I experienced pain and fear that no one should ever go through.

Besides being violent, that devil engaged in criminal activity, including car theft and buying and selling stolen goods. There were times when he didn't have a "getaway driver" so he made me the driver. I had no choice! These runs were done in the middle of the night and he always carried a gun.

During this time we lived in an apartment in Franklin Square, New York. It was where my daughter Lisa was born, an Aquarian. She was an easy baby to care for. Living there was a nightmare because of all of the continued abuse that took place. Dan would get mad about something—you never knew what, and would push me down to the floor and kick me—it didn't matter to him if I was pregnant or not. I was always worried that Lisa would become another victim in his sick rituals of torture.

It seemed he stayed away from her and concentrated on Tee and me.

From there we moved to Grand Central Garden Apartments in Bellerose, NY. It was here that, nineteen months after Lisa was born, Kelly came into our world, a Leo. Kelly was another beautiful baby with a smile that lit up the room. The girls are nineteen months apart in age. It was here that I finally found a group of friends and a sense of community. We did things together and the comradery helped me to deal with the abuse and criminal activity that was taking place at home. One of these women, Nan, would become a life-long friend.

Next, Dan bought a house in West Hempstead, New York, without telling me about it, and put it in his name only. It was a lovely Tudor home. Despite being a beautiful house lots of horrible, brutal things happened there to all of us. The house had a very long, narrow, gravel driveway that turned into a warning system. The kids and I always knew to listen to the speed and sound of the way Dan would pull his van into the driveway. The way the gravel sounded was different when he was in a drunken state in contrast to when he drove in normally. This was how we would judge how drunk Dan was and if we needed to hide and pretend we were sleeping. When we heard the sound, we would all run into different areas of the house and as far away from him as possible. We would not go near him—no matter what. The driveway gave us a head start to find safety. To this day we all say the same thing about the gravel driveway. It was our friend and savior.

For so many years, I and my children lived in constant fear for our lives. Existing in this environment robbed us of our joy and replaced it with a wounded spirit that was not allowed to heal before more pain was heaped upon it. I have sustained multiple broken bones at the hands of a man that should have been my shield against the world and my protector. The beautiful Tudor house in West Hempstead where we lived had become a prison. There were too many threatening incidents to recall, but some brought me dangerously close to serious injury and death. These were the ones that finally gave me the courage to escape.

One such incident occurred late one night when we were alerted by the crunching sounds of tires on the gravel driveway. We heard the devil arrive home drunk—as he did on many nights. I jumped into bed and pretended I was asleep. The two girls, Lisa and Kelly, did the same. He staggered into our master bedroom intent on tormenting me; cursing out loud about how he should kill me. I was trembling under the covers, so much so that I thought he would see the vibration and know I wasn't asleep. He took one of his decorative swords off the wall and put the tip into my back. While he was putting pressure on it he kept repeating, "I should stab you and kill you right now." He was saying it over and over again. I thought that was the night I would lose my life. Who would protect the kids? I prayed to Jesus that he wouldn't go and kill them after he killed me. The fear was intense. Finally he just passed out on the bed. There were angels over us that night protecting us as they would again and again, on many other nights.

The only positive thing Dan did was to pay for me to go to nursing school to get my licensed practical nurse (LPN) license. It was a one-year program. He hired a full-time babysitter to take care of the kids—we now had two daughters along with Tee (at my parents' house) while I was in school. I graduated, took my boards and passed, and had my nursing license. It was the nicest thing he has ever done for me. I didn't use it during our marriage, but it was there when I needed it much later on.

I often ask myself that one lingering question. Why did I stay so long? The answers are complex and suffice to say that poor self-esteem and a lack of my own source of income and a place to escape to, along with my concern for my children's well-being and the constant wearing down of my resolve, were all contributing factors. Like feet sinking rapidly into ocean-drenched sand, I was stuck in a deep hole that I couldn't dig myself out of; the more the waves crashed, the deeper I sank.

I thought many times of escaping, but escape takes courage and most of the time I didn't have the courage or knowledge to actually pull it off. Not only did I not possess the know-how, I was scared to death to even think about it and the consequences of the decision. Dan always told me if I left he would find me and kill me along with anyone else with me and I believed him. I certainly knew he was capable. Most of the time freedom was only a fantasy that I dreamed about but never actually believed. Sometimes I found myself daydreaming about how to kill him while he was sleeping. That would also be a way of escape but of course it too was a fantasy that

I never went through with. Living with him for ten years had turned me into someone I didn't like.

Finally, after nine years of marriage and living in fear every day, I began devising a plan of escape. But while I was fleshing it out, as luck would have it, Dan got into a very bad motorcycle accident. A car broadsided him, threw him off the bike, and the handlebars went into his head. He suffered a traumatic brain injury. He had just bought a brand new bicentennial Harley-Davidson motorcycle, and it was his first time riding it—the bike was stunning. I was supposed to be with him on the back of the Harley that night but plans changed. The bike was totaled and he wound up in a coma. When I drove by the accident site there was an outline of his body on the street. No one believed he was going to survive. As a side note, while I was in the hospital waiting room, my sister arrived out of the blue, crying and distraught after hearing about the accident. I thought it was a bit strange at the time, given our relationship wasn't close, but it would all make sense later on.

Dan was in a coma for one week and when he woke up he had a lot of difficulty with daily living, such as speaking, dressing, and feeding himself. All those skills he lost and needed a lot of rehabilitation to get them back. I don't remember how long he was in the hospital but this accident and recovery turned an already violent man even more dangerous. He couldn't work and make money and that made him angrier than ever. Even in his condition, he would chase me around the house with weapons—whatever he got his hands on—and would pull the wires out of my car so I couldn't use my vehicle, to keep me in the house. I kept thinking; why didn't he die? It would have been so much easier. And why didn't I seize the opportunity to leave when I had the chance? My escape was handed to me with no advance planning on my part, yet instead of running, I stayed to take care of him. I can't believe at the time I thought *how could I leave a person, no matter how bad, alone to recuperate?* What was I thinking? I wasn't thinking! I was suffering from Stockholm syndrome. At the time, I prayed I didn't make the wrong decision—but of course I did! My empathetic impulse was misdirected and left me vulnerable to even more abuse. In the end I would live to regret my decision.

There were things I did during these ten years that still haunt me, although I have come to realize they were done for survival by a woman who had been battered to the point where she was not, as I've stated, thinking clearly. One such mistake was what I termed the "Get even tour." It was a time during which I engaged in multiple affairs and sexual encounters in an attempt to get back at the devil for his infidelity. Ultimately I was the one to pay the price as it resulted in five needless abortions in order to hide the resulting pregnancies from Dan, who by this time had received a vasectomy and, being of a murderous mindset, had he gotten wind of any of them it would have meant certain death for me.

The final straw came the night the devil pulled into the gravel driveway like a bat out of hell. We heard the key click open the back door and his footsteps as he entered the house. There was no time to run. The girls were in the bathroom washing their feet. Kelly was sitting on the sink with her feet in it and Lisa was standing in front of the sink with one foot in it. Dan came immediately into the bathroom looking for trouble—he was drunk. He began teasing the girls and neither one was in the mood. Lisa was able to escape the bathroom—she was slick—but Kelly was trapped in there with him. I went into the bathroom to free Kelly. Kelly was mad and talking back and that's something you never do and get away with. I had to get the girls away from him or something bad was going to happen. The girls managed to leave the bathroom and Dan cornered them in the den, grabbing both of them by the throat and squeezing hard. Shortly they were turning blue and I knew they were in mortal trouble. I had to get them away so I intervened from behind. I don't remember exactly how, but he dropped his hold on them. He broke glass on the floor seeing that they were barefoot to slow them down and resume the torture. I yelled, "Run downstairs!" They knew I meant to our downstairs tenant, Rosalie, who was our intermittent protector. We all ran down to her apartment in the basement and locked ourselves in. Dan came down banging on the door but we never opened it. He wouldn't stop until I agreed to come out. I left the girls in Rosalie's care for the rest of the night. What happened when I went upstairs with Dan? I have no memory of what took place and had to rely on my daughter Lisa's memory—she was nine years old at the time—to fill in the details.

That night, I determined we had to leave or we would soon be dead. His physical outbursts in the past had always been directed toward Tee or me—never the girls. This time he lashed out at his own daughters. He nearly killed them, but he appeared to have no awareness. I knew this was the moment to escape because next time we might not be so lucky. It was the turning point in this decade of madness and the moment when I realized there would be no savior to ride in on a white horse. It was up to me to rescue myself and my girls or eventually we would all wind up nothing more than a tragedy on tomorrow's front-page news.

One of my affairs was the means through which we were able to make our escape. I'm ashamed to say I used this man's affections for my benefit, but he owned a truck and was willing to do whatever I asked. I knew leading him on wasn't right but I needed his help to pull it off and wasn't in a position to judge the morality of my actions—I was a desperate woman. Once I made the decision, I confided with my friend Rose, who helped me arrange a place of escape, and little by little over time, I packed our clothing and the things we were going to take with us. I put them in Rosalie's apartment for safekeeping. Dan never found out, thank God! The plan was almost complete except for the "when." I didn't have much time.

On the designated day, we loaded our personal belongings onto this sweet man's truck, I left a note for Dan, and we drove down that gravel driveway to freedom. Ultimately, that gravel driveway, the one that served as a warning over those painful ten years, would serve as the pathway through which we were delivered from our old life into the safety of a new one—one in which we would eventually thrive rather than simply survive.

Dan was determined to turn me into a victim, to crush my spirit, and make me think I was of no value—and it worked! I endured it for ten long years, and the steady diet of negativity imposed its intended effect. I was rendered powerless to change my situation and had allowed a bellicose man with criminal tendencies to define who I was—and after hearing how worthless I was so often, I began to believe it too. What I didn't know at the time, and didn't learn until much later, was that our opinions are not formed in a vacuum of one's own mind, but rather they are influenced by the opinions of the people that surround us—and my people and their opinions were overwhelmingly negative. Since then I have learned that I am not defined by other people's wrong opinions of me or by my own distorted opinions of myself, but rather I am a child of destiny, and my path was written before I was born.

For many years I'd suddenly experience moments that my mind would transport me back to those frightening days and I would shake with fear. It was PTSD—the aftereffects of my abuse kicking in. I'd look over my shoulders in both directions and anxiety would replace the tranquility of the moment. I would be unable to stop it, yet I'd learned to expect it. It could have been the sound of tires crushing gravel or the slow pounding of footsteps. Whatever it happened to be, it appeared like a serpent in a basket once the lid had been opened and it slithered out. After so many instances I no longer tried to force the lid back on. Rather, I took it as a reminder that I'd traveled a long road from that Tudor house of horrors and that I am no longer that weak person and am proud that my family and I have persevered and have ultimately overcome.

CHAPTER 5

PORT WASHINGTON, AUGUST 1977: FIRST YEAR OF FREEDOM AND THE HIPPIE LIFE

M y spiritual healing began the day I moved to Port Washington, New York, in August 1977. I was thirty years old and my children and I were going to start a new life. Port Washington is a one-square-mile town that sits atop a 120-foot bluff on the North Shore, which is on the coast of the Long Island Sound. It is literally surrounded by beaches and hills. The houses are old Victorian with many listed on the National Register of Historic Places. It was a town filled with Russians and hippies at the time. There was a new age vibe, in spite of the old world charm. It was a welcoming place and the girls and I felt comfortable there. The town and its people were some of the most loving I have ever met. I learned a new way of life and was introduced to spirituality and a loving, healthy lifestyle. It was just what I needed.

After the escape, we settled into a house with new friends, Judy and Jack. They were our saviors, allowing us to use their home as our refuge and residence until I could figure out what my next move would be. There was much to work out. Leaving the devil was an enormous feat which took a physical and emotional toll on all of us. I figured the rest should be downhill. That was far from the truth, as the hard part of crafting a life was just now beginning. It was time for me to take control, get a job, and get us on the right path. I had a nursing license, thank God, but I never had a real nursing job. I was scared to death.

Judy and Jack were supportive and with their encouragement, we persevered. I began to view Judy as a soulmate and believed that we had traveled together in other lives. They had a son, who was two years old at that time. Tee was living with my parents and was going to the nearby school and we chose not to move him again so that he could maintain a safe and consistent life. I felt he was in a good place with my parents.

Many of the people in the community were musicians, artists, and all sorts of creative people. They were into healthy eating and that's where I began to rethink my eating habits, opting for more organic produce, and questioning vaccines and their safety. It was a time to reassess my life's goals and the direction I and my children would take. It was also a time for pursuing my creative side. I started taking guitar lessons from Rose, my goomah who helped me find safety. We played guitar and did some singing together. Singing had been my passion from an early age. I used to sing Madame Butterfly's aria as a little girl in my mother's closet. Finally, at this place in this time, I was free to sing my heart out.

Rose and I were a good balance for each other. I was an Aquarian and she was a Leo. On the astrological chart we are one hundred and eighty degrees apart, which is an opposition. With oppositions we give each other what we lack.

One afternoon, Rose took me into Manhattan to the Ansonia Hotel for a singing class. I was very nervous because I had never sung in front of anyone. If I had a closet it would have felt better. We walked into class; our teacher was a woman that clearly had psychic ability and knew exactly what the students needed just by looking at them. I felt even more afraid because I knew I was going to be called upon, which was my worst fear; I chose Carole King's "It's too Late" to perform. Rose went up to sing first. The teacher told her to sit on a stool in front of the class and speak the words while showing no emotion. She didn't want any theatrics. Rose found it impossible to do that. While Rose was an amazing performer, she was unable to do what was asked. The teacher told her to sit back down in her chair. That was a profound moment for me. Seeing how Rose, the most outgoing person I knew, could not pull back and speak the song, as performing was natural to her. It was now my turn. The teacher told me to sing it as I practiced it. So I did so—trying to get the right amount of air while attempting to keep my body from shaking. I'm sure I didn't sound very good. In the end I was able to complete the task and I felt proud. She then asked me to sing the song again, this time dancing all around the room. I died inside; not only did I have to sing the song again but I now had to perform the song. Something I had never done in my life but always dreamed of doing. Somehow I got the courage and did what she asked. I sang the song dancing all around the room. Again I was terrified, but I felt good about myself. I thought by now I should be done and ran back to my seat, only to hear her ask me to sing the song again, looking into one of the male students' eyes. I was beyond mortified but again I persevered and completed the task. It was a life-changing moment of self-awareness for me that ushered in my journey to come out of my shell and face my fears no matter how uncomfortable the situation.

The girls and I took over the basement and were very comfortable and appreciative for the hospitality given to us. Lisa and Kelly were happy and found all kinds of friends, some of whom are still friends today. I had no money to speak of, and knew I wasn't going to get any from Dan, except his minimal support money, thirty dollars a week per child, and fifteen hundred dollars in cash in one lump sum, but what I did have was an LPN license. That was my ace in the hole. True, I had no real nursing experience, and little confidence, but it would prove to be the catalyst for the thirty-six-year nursing career that had previously only been a far-off dream.

I applied for jobs in nursing homes in the area and landed a position as an LPN in Forest Glen HRF. It was in an assisted living facility located ten minutes from my house and I loved it. Specifically, I loved the seniors and wanted to advocate for them. My heart cried out that this was the right road. This facility and job was my jump off point that set the path for my career and life in a direction of independence both professionally and financially. Continuing to improve the lives of our family was what motivated me to work hard. I needed to be able to take care of my children and this led to an increase in my personal self-worth. I was determined to be totally self-sufficient and to never be caught in a "no way out" situation ever again.

While I was busy establishing a new life for us, I was also in the middle of a divorce from the devil. Finally, on December 9, 1977, my divorce was granted based on "cruel and inhuman treatment." Excerpts from the divorce papers read as follows:

> Defendant has without cause, burst into outbursts of temper, addressing plaintiff in vile, abusive and threatening language, frequently culminating in throwing objects about and at the plaintiff, and in actual assaults upon her, kicking, slapping, punching, choking and throwing her about.

> In October, the defendant was intoxicated, he threw plaintiff to the bed, punching her on the back and sides causing a rib fracture. In February 1973, the defendant threw a plate at her, which struck her in the ribs and caused another fracture. Also in February 1977, he was observed striking an infant in a cruel and vicious manner causing great pain and the child becoming hysterical.

I was granted full custody of the kids, thirty dollars support money per child per week and no alimony. I was also granted twelve to fifteen hundred dollars, in one lump sum—nothing else. I asked for no alimony from him because most of his money was connected to something shady and I wanted nothing from Dan but my freedom.

One year after our escape to a new life, we secured our own apartment on a beautiful street in Port Washington, with a view of the Long Island Sound. Freedom was finally ours; it felt real, smelled sweet, and tasted divine. As the song "Feeling Good" says,

> *Birds flying high you know how I feel*
> *Sun in the sky you know how I feel*
> *Breeze driftin' on by you know how I feel*
> *It's a new dawn*
> *It's a new day*
> *It's a new life for me*
> *And I'm feeling good (Newley and Bricusse 1964)*

I was beginning to sense the possibility of a brand new life and was going to do my best to soar high and claim my share of the sky.

CHAPTER 6

THE DEVIL AND HIS DISCIPLE: MY SISTER REPLACES ME

While I was on the launchpad preparing to soar, unbeknownst to me, three weeks after our escape, while we were reestablishing our lives in Port Washington, and I was securing a new job, I was hit with a bombshell of news that nearly shook me to my core.

Word came through the grapevine that Maggie and Dan had hooked up. The story was he was looking for me and went to her house to see if she knew where I was—which she didn't. They were crying on each other's shoulders when one thing led to another. The next thing anybody knew, she had left her second husband, taken her two young sons with her, and moved into what had been my prison—the house in West Hempstead—with him! *Well, this explains her performance in the hospital waiting room when Dan nearly died*, I surmised. No one can prepare for this type of sibling betrayal. I expected the worst from Dan, but my sister?! I was shocked and hurt. Although we weren't close, she's blood. Why would my sister betray me? Upon hearing the news, my PTSD reared its ugly head and I began to shake with fear once again. I had just freed myself from this violent man and now my sister had dragged him right back into our family and my life. The devil was now my future brother-in-law and our children's "uncle-daddy." I grew chilled at the very thought of coming face to face with this man who treated me so violently—at family gatherings. How would my family respond to this unholy alliance?

The two demons were now a team and I would have to either accept it or avoid any contact with family in the future. It was an awkward dynamic with no real solution. It was 1978 and to complicate matters, my mother, aware of the entire messy situation, had just written me a deathbed letter months before she died of colon cancer. In it she begged me to hold the family together because I was the strong one. *Suddenly I was the strong one?* She also said that maybe it was a blessing that Maggie was with Dan. This way I would have no problem getting my support money because she would make sure that everything was done correctly. A request from my beloved mother on her deathbed was powerful and impacted me greatly. How could I ignore it? So, with my mother's words ringing in my ears, and despite the hurt and betrayal I felt, it seemed I had little choice but to do whatever I could to make peace for my mother's sake.

CHAPTER 7

THE LETTER: MY MOTHER'S DEATHBED REQUEST

My mother was not in the habit of writing me letters, but on this particular day, in bed, terminally ill with colon cancer, she pushed an envelope into my palm without saying a word. I intuitively knew it was a letter of some sort and that it was important. I began to tense up as I slipped it into my purse. What was it about? I did not know, but as I left her room and drove home, my mind streamed through a list of possibilities.

Once at home, I set the letter on the table but did not open it. I'd look over at it periodically and it appeared to be magnifying in intensity with each glance. Intuitively I knew it contained words that would alter my life and I began to feel anxiety creeping in. Was it a confession? If so, what was this secret that was left to a deathbed letter? I had known about her boyfriend, John, for years—it was an open secret. What else could it be? I was at a loss. By the second day, I had finally summoned enough courage to unseal the envelope and read its contents. I can't remember most of the actual words she used except to say that she was depending on **me** to bring our fractured family together once she was gone. Our family was always fragmented—it was nothing new, but on a deeper level, as a mother, I understood. The real mystery was why she said, "Nancy, you are the strong one." She knew my past. *How am I the strong one?* I thought.

By "family," my mother meant my relationship with my sister and the impossible situation she created with Dan. She was aware of what took place—as was everyone in my life, both family and friends. She also stated that "having my sister in control of the child support money would make my life easier." Well, I didn't hold out hope for that given her betrayal. About the only thing I could hope for was that she would act as a buffer so that I wouldn't have to interact directly with Dan to get the child support checks—a confrontation I was happy to avoid as he had left Maggie in charge of handling the money and was never present when I arrived.

Still, a deathbed letter from my mother trusting me with bringing the family together held power and my reaction to it ranged from initial anger for saddling me with this burden, to wondering why she chose me in the first place, to finally, a vow to do what she asked. In the end, she had tasked me with keeping the family together and I made it my mission to do just that. So, to honor my mother's wish, I was compelled to spend the next twenty-five years trying to reconcile us into one cohesive happy family.

CHAPTER 8

UNCLE-DADDY AND
THE NEW NORMAL

In the beginning of this new family dynamic, the normal rules flew out the window. Dan was the girls' father, but since he was now married to their Aunt Maggie, he was occupying the position designated for an uncle? It was all too confusing. The girls took to calling Dan their "uncle-daddy." What could I say?

I would drive Lisa and Kelly over to the house in West Hempstead. I needed to pick up the support check and sometimes I left the girls there. As I pulled into the gravel driveway for the first time post-escape, the horrors of the property came flooding back. I thought to myself, *What the hell am I doing here?* I already knew the answer—I needed the meager support money for our survival. As I was driving, I was also honoring and thanking the gravel driveway for protecting us all those years. I told myself the girls would be okay left alone with my sister, but the experiences my girls shared gave me pause.

There would be days Maggie would have her church friends—nuns and elders—over when I arrived to pick up the child support check. She would ask me to tell my daughters not to call me Mom in front of them. I interpreted this to mean she was embarrassed by the way she wound up living in my old house and married to my former husband and didn't want the good church folks to know the real story. I thought to myself, *How can they not see that she's the devil's disciple?* The irony of this "white glove" scene playing out with the church folks in the Tudor House of Horrors left me in disbelief—it was a black comedy worthy of Hollywood. Tell my daughters not to call me Mom! I wasn't going to do it—not for Maggie and not even to satisfy my dear mother's deathbed request. No one was going to make me deny my motherhood for the sake of appearances. It was something I could not abide and eventually it caught up with her and like most lies, the truth eventually came spewing out.

Instead of helping the kids and me, Maggie only made things worse. She would try and separate the girls and me by bad-mouthing me to them. They were young and vulnerable after having a life of violence with their father. Maggie worked on them for many years. She would ask them to live with her so she could adopt them. She also told them that the support money their father gave me was their money. The girls wanted to believe her and after a weekend of brainwashing would come home with an attitude and would need to be reprogrammed. Maggie began a pattern of withholding the money, wouldn't mail it, as agreed, and had many excuses why she didn't put it in the mail. She took over the whole support money issue; Dan simply washed his hands of it. I would have to drive to West Hempstead (forty minutes away) and pick up the check if I wanted it on time. She made it very difficult and I never understood why. So my mother's theory of Maggie making it better for me was all wrong, yet her words lingered in my ear while I tried to pursue some form of a relationship with Maggie and Dan—and hating every minute of it.

As for whether Dan was abusing Maggie as he did me, no one ever knew. Knowing my sister, she would have responded to him much differently than I did. I can visualize Maggie cowering and crying, which might have been her saving grace—while I stood silent. Dan took my silence as defiance and in his mind, defiance was something that needed to be crushed.

It's true, Dan had crushed my spirit, but now I was moving forward. As for where I was headed, it was unclear, but one thing was certain; I was now going forward into my future instead of fleeing from my past, and while I proceeded without clarity, little did I know the universe had already prepared the way for me.

CHAPTER 9

MY KNIGHT IN
FADED BLUE JEANS:
FINDING MY SOULMATE

It was now May 1978 and we were settled in and beginning our new life in Port Washington. The last thing I wanted to do was to go back to West Hempstead, where I experienced so much pain, but my friend Rose had a different idea. She said, "Let's go back to West Hempstead; I'm missing our friends there." Yesterday's News was the neighborhood bar that we hung out at with the devil and his friends, when I was living with him. It was a Sunday afternoon and I had my two girls with me, Lisa and Kelly. Rose was with her husband and her daughter. My daughters and Rose's daughter were great friends then and now. I was reluctant—who wants to go back to a place of hurt?—but there were also a lot of good friends who took care of me. Rose, being a persuasive person, won out and we took this serendipitous, life-changing day trip.

It was a fun visit with the girls playing pool and video games. I saw many old friends that began as Dan's friends and became mine. Ryan Shore, a dear friend and a wonderful guy, even though he was a drug dealer and a heroin user, as were many of the guys in this bar, introduced me to Tom, the new bartender. Tom seemed to be a really nice guy and we had an immediate attraction to each other. It was both mysterious and powerful. If love at first sight is real then this was it. Tom and I and Rose and Greg sat in a booth and Rose and Tom did most of the talking. Greg and I were the quiet ones. I felt comfortable with this new outgoing bartender, so I just listened. Tom was my type and I intuitively thought he was trustworthy. Being intrigued, I didn't say a word; I simply listened to his conversation with Rose. When it came time to go home Tom looked at me and said, "I'm going home with you, right?" I said yes, without hesitation.

As I reflect on this moment I realize it seems like a dangerous thing to do in today's world, but it was a time of free love, and I was a hippie living a free-spirited life. Rose took the girls home with her for a sleepover. That was the start of a whirlwind romance that has lasted over forty years. Tee was thirteen, and the girls, Lisa and Kelly, were nine and eight at the time.

Soon after, Tom moved in with us into my apartment in Port Washington. We never really thought it through. It all happened so fast. We were madly in love and wanted to be together. He had no problem with my history and children. It was a brave move on his part and I would have understood if he ran as fast as he could away from us but he never did no matter how tough it got. He wanted to be a father to the kids but he didn't know how; still he was going to give it a try. He always tried to be supportive. He was a kind and decent man, something I was not used to. My history with choosing men had a poor track record, so I figured the universe stepped in and found me a good one; someone who would honor and encourage me, for which I am forever grateful. Tom was a beautiful soul; he loved and adored me, and told me how beautiful I was. What more could I ask for? Yes, we struggled, but we did it together as a team. He helped with the kids and knew they were wounded as we both were.

It was stressful nurturing a new relationship along with raising kids. It was just Lisa and Kelly. Tee was still living at my mother's house. The girls were difficult because they didn't approve of our relationship. Since I had to work, Tom was the babysitter. The kids resented his discipline. It was a big problem. As I think back, it was too soon after the devil for the kids to adjust, but I was still naive and unaware. I also needed to go to work and couldn't afford a babysitter. I made more money at the time so it was economically smarter for me to work and for Tom to stay home. I was following a pattern my mother set when she introduced me to her boyfriend at an early age; bringing Tom home so quickly didn't seem to be a bad thing at the moment.

Not long after our relationship started, Tom thought it would be a good time to bring Tee home with us. I was concerned about all the changes in his and our lives and that shifting him again would be harmful, but my mother had just been diagnosed with colon cancer and was given an eight-month prognosis, so given that development, the time seemed right to bring Tee back into the fold. Tee seemed to have no difficulties with the new situation. He

45

got along well with Tom and didn't give us any problems with our relationship.

Being the hippies we were, there was always a lot of pot flowing through the house. The kids knew we smoked and we smoked in front of them with our friends. It was normal in our circles, so the kids grew up with pot around. Again, I wasn't thinking it was a problem. Or was it?

The more I learned about Tom, the more endeared I was to this imperfect man that rescued us. Tom was brought up by a verbally abusive, alcoholic father and a passive, depressed mother who was too wounded to love her children. He was one of three boys and was the middle child. He expressed that he never felt love or support from his parents. His father was overly critical and this negativity affected Tom's self-esteem. His father was verbally abusive to everyone in the house including his mother. His mother had a severe anxiety disorder, was a breast cancer survivor, and was taking Valium to help her cope. So you see, Tom was struggling with his own demons. Once Tom was of age, he was drafted into the army in October 1969. He was sent to Vietnam in January and served there from January 1971 to October 1971. His psychological tests prior to deployment revealed him to be empathetic, so he was assigned to work in the military hospital. While in Vietnam he worked with the community and civilians in the hospital, which was an old school turned into a medical facility. When he got stateside he worked at Walter Reed Hospital caring for all the war wounded. As an orthopedic technician, he saw horrendous war wounds including amputees that had their limbs shot or blown off by a bomb. He gave good care to these veterans and is proud of the work he did there. After our marriage, Tom completed college and found his place working with the mentally ill. He began as a therapy aide and worked his way up the ladder to become Treatment Team Leader at Pilgrim State Psychiatric Hospital.

After his discharge from the Army, he married his first wife, Mona. Theirs was a volatile marriage from the beginning that led to a lot of pain and resulted in a divorce after four years. He was in the process of this long divorce when we met.

Despite having found a good man who was on my side, I allowed outside forces to influence our relationship. It all began about two months into our relationship. My landlord didn't like that Tom was living in the apartment and gave us a hard time. She wanted us to move out. At that point my stress was at maximum level, with the girls and now my landlord putting pressure on me about Tom. How did I react? I threw Tom out of the house with nowhere to go. I didn't think about him at all, as I was focused on the other hundred things I was dealing with in my state of survival mode. I was pregnant again and didn't know how to deal with everything that was being heaped on me and being pregnant didn't help. Tom went back to West Hempstead where he worked and rented an attic room in a friend's house. He had no furniture or bed, just a hammock on the floor where he slept. We stayed separated for two months until I came to my senses and realized I had let go of the man who loved me deeply. After two months we got back together and have been lovingly together ever since.

We moved out of Port Washington and just five minutes away into Glen Cove after we got back together. That's where I gave birth to Casey. We lived in that house for a year when the landlord asked us to leave because Lisa and Kelly tortured him and his family with verbal assaults and mischief. One day he came to our door and said, "I love you guys, but the girls are awful and we can't take them anymore, so you have to leave." So, back we went to Port Washington and rented a house.

Casey Sloan was born on March 19, 1979, a Pisces. Number four for me and number one for Tom. What a precious gift from heaven. She was beautiful and we bonded immediately. I got pregnant with Casey within one month of Tom moving in. Unlike my five previous pregnancies, I never once thought about aborting this baby because I was finally in a loving relationship and was looking forward to a child with Tom.

When Casey was a year old, Tom and I decided to get married. We were married by a Unitarian minister and held our ceremony in the park next door and the party at our house. My friend Rose played a James Taylor song on her guitar as Tom and I walked into the park. It was beautiful surrounded by all our family and friends. I did a lot of the cooking as friends pitched in. A friend from work even made the wedding cake.

Thinking I was getting married and not being pregnant, I was thrilled—as this would be the first time. It didn't last long; I found out I was pregnant again with my fifth child, and I was pregnant when I got married. No surprise! This was my pattern. I gave birth to Seth Thomas Sloan on

January 20, 1981, an Aquarian. His was the easiest birth and he was nine pounds eight ounces; another beautiful baby that we fell in love with immediately. We were going to name him Zed until the last minute; we changed it to Seth Thomas because that was the name of the clock on the delivery room wall.

Ultimately, Tom was my knight in shining armor. He provided the emotional security we needed. He protected my heart and cherished me and the children. No, he didn't ride up on a white horse clad in shiny metal; instead, he was a real man who came into my life at a time when I needed him and swept me away with real love. Now that we were married, was I going to have a normal relationship? Would I have someone to be around to support me and my children? Would I have a partner to share my life with and to love and be loved by? I was beginning to think the answer was yes!

CHAPTER 10

MY PROFESSIONAL LIFE BEGINS: CLIMBING THE LADDER, 1977–2001

I had a dream when I was a little girl. I remember being five years old and announcing to my parents, "I want to be a nurse and help other people when I grow up." What confidence I exuded back then! I knew exactly what I wanted. As the years passed, I continued to hold that dream close to my heart, but like all dreams deferred, with the passage of time it began to slip away. A lack of confidence and dedication on my part resulted in my dream evaporating into the ether. Two marriages and three children later I was left in survival mode, struggling to make it from day to day with no time to pursue my dream career of becoming a registered nurse.

Once in Port Washington, my LPN license allowed me to land my first job in a health facility. The owner was Tony Manzo, a wealthy, self-made man. He started out in the construction business and bought land in Glen Cove, Long Island, in a medical plaza where he built two facilities, side by side—one a nursing home and one a health-related facility (HRF). Nursing homes have sicker residents and the regulations are more strict than HRFs'. HRF residents can care for themselves with assistance taking medications, serving meals, and other activities of daily living. I was hired to work at Forest Glen HRF for the Elderly.

Manzo would become my friend, mentor, and spiritual advisor for many years to come. He guided me through tough times in my personal and professional life. Manzo took a liking to me right away and wanted to teach me everything he knew. He saw possibility in me that I didn't see in for myself. I was thrilled to learn everything he could teach—at that point I was a blank slate ready to absorb all the knowledge that was presented to me. I opened myself up to what seemed like a far reaching goal of one day running the entire facility. I envisioned improving the administrative policies and how they would lead to a more efficient, resident-centered facility. I just had to pay my dues, learn as much as possible, and eventually get my registered nurse license in order to take full charge of staff and policy. This became my new dream and the road that I was destined to take. The key was to get my RN license.

I was working as hard as I could—double shifts and holidays—as my immediate goal was to secure an apartment in Port Washington. I loved the town and work was just minutes away. As a family we wanted to stay in the area. We had made friends close by and were very comfortable. But there was no room in my life to go to college to pursue my education yet.

That all changed during my second year at Forest Glen when I met Tom, my third husband and soulmate. We fell in love at first sight. With Tom as a stabilizing force, I was able to begin to chase my dream. In a secure relationship, I could finally think past survival mode and focus seriously on acquiring the education I needed to become an RN and pursue my ultimate career goal of becoming a director of nursing. With Manzo as my mentor and Tom's encouragement, which I leaned into because his confidence in me far exceeded my own, I began to believe that my once-deferred dream could actually become a reality.

In the meantime, Manzo told me if I got my RN license, after a few years he would promote me to the director of nursing. It was an opportunity that seemed beyond my grasp at that time, but one that motivated me and that I clung to tenaciously as a goal for the future. The nagging question had always been, "How am I going to ever go to school and get my RN license living paycheck to paycheck with no money left over?" It seemed at that time to be out of reach, but I never stopped dreaming. Manzo had presented me with a pathway to success and I knew I eventually had to walk it in order to seize the opportunity.

Seeing elderly residents, most who needed so much and being deprived of adequate care, touched me and served as another motivating factor for me to succeed. It was during this time that I realized that I needed to be part of the change and that it was my calling to get involved. Acquiring my RN license became my primary and urgent goal. The real question was how in the world would I pull it off?

The opportunity presented itself in 1985 when I had an opportunity to apply for a scholarship to get my nursing degree through the union with which I was affiliated through work. I had to take some exams, but in the end I was granted the scholarship. I had a choice whether I wanted a diploma, an associate's degree, or the full bachelor's degree in nursing. It was a huge decision to consider because I now had five children and the task of school seemed impossible to accomplish. I still carried a lot of insecurity issues which played a role in my hesitation. I kept trying to talk myself out of it, but Tom continued to encourage me to do it and kept telling me that I was smarter than I thought I was. He told me he would pick up the slack at home and that we could accomplish my dream as a team. I knew that I would need a bachelor's degree in order to carry out my dream, so that's what I chose. He was willing to work more at home and wouldn't grant me much space to think negative thoughts. I finally had a man who wanted to make a life with me!

There were some requirements that were hard on me. I had to attend school in the Bronx at Lehman College, which was a two-hour drive each way on the worst highways you can imagine. I wasn't allowed to work so I could focus on my studies, and I received a stipend of two hundred dollars a week, tax free. The union would continue to pay my medical insurance, my seniority was maintained, and my books, uniforms, and tuition were paid for. How could I pass this up? Here was my chance and it dropped into my lap at exactly the right moment.

I was still worried about how we would make it without my regular paycheck, as two hundred dollars a week wouldn't go far. Tom kept encouraging me that we had to sacrifice temporarily, but the payoff would be huge for the family and for my dream. It felt good to have someone support me so strongly and not allow my insecurities to get in the way. We took out student loans and somehow we made it.

Driving to the Bronx every day was unpleasant, but I knew it was only temporary. For four years I loved school and I thrived in the environment. I started to come out of my shell. I became one of the class leaders and discovered that Tom was right; I was pretty smart after all. I never would have believed it, but pursuing my education revealed strengths in me I never knew I had; the same strengths that Manzo had seen when he hired me. In high school I never did earn good grades and passed each year by the skin of my teeth. It's no wonder considering my home environment, right? In contrast, I graduated college cum laude with a 3.5 GPA and my Bachelor of Science degree in Nursing. There was much more at stake this time around and I took school seriously. I received many department awards at graduation, including the Faculty Award, given by the professors to a student who made a difference. I was member of the nursing honor society. My self-esteem soared during this time and I was beginning to see myself for who I really was and what I was capable of. I became comfortable speaking in front of groups and liked who I was becoming. I knew I had a long way to go, but I was on my path. Not only did school allow me to move forward toward independence and follow my dreams, it showed me a whole new side of myself that I liked. I was creating an entirely new life for myself—with Tom's help—while the old life was quickly becoming a faded memory.

Nine months before I graduated, I got pregnant with number six, a boy, Ryan, born on June 8, 1989, a Gemini. My graduation date was June 1, 1989. It was tough going through my last year of school pregnant. I wanted this baby to wait until I graduated, and he did—my sweet Ryan. Soon after I gave birth I took the nursing boards and passed and now I was really on my way. I continued to climb the ladder, building on my foundation one rung at a time.

I returned to Forest Glen after graduation. Now, with the credentials I needed, I was qualified to enter the supervisor/management lane. True to his word, Manzo made me a supervisor right away. Being responsible for staff was my next phase of development. I needed this piece to learn how to be the problem solver on my shift. I loved being a supervisor and was good at it. I worked about a year in that position when Manzo approached me to promote me to director of nursing. I was scared to death. I had very little supervisory experience and didn't feel confident yet. He reassured me he would be with me every step of the way, so with hesitation I accepted his offer. This was going to be one of the biggest challenges of my life. Baptism by fire was about to happen.

I took over the director of nursing position for two and a half years. I did a good job but I always felt like I was missing something, and I was! I was missing more extended experience before managing at this level. Experience is required to build a strong foundation. Experience prepares you to be a strong leader once you reach the top and are in control. I had a great team around me that made me look good, yet I knew that wasn't enough. I learned so much but I knew I needed to take a step back before stepping into this important role again. The thought of leaving Manzo was breaking my heart, but I needed to make a move so that I could be the most effective director possible. In 1994, I was offered a position as an assistant director of nursing at a well-established nursing home in the area.

As I mentioned, nursing homes were a lot more difficult to run due to stricter regulations and more complicated care issues. The residents are significantly more deteriorated than those in an HRF. Since I only had experience in an HRF, I knew I had a difficult road of learning ahead. I also knew this position would fill in the gaps in my training and preparation that I was missing. Manzo had promoted me from LPN to RN supervisor and within a year to director of nursing. I skipped an all-important step working as an assistant to the director. That's where you learn the ropes. It was difficult to leave Manzo, but he knew I needed to go and learn. I hoped maybe one day I could go back to work for him. I will never forget him and his generosity and belief in me, and we continued to stay in touch for many years.

I lasted at the new facility for just nine months. I was unable to fit into the owner's way of doing business and was uncomfortable with the unethical requirements that the management team asked of me. So, just as I was getting my feet wet in the field and gaining a lot of important learning, I resigned. I moved on to another facility to help them out with their care plan system. That turned out to be my specialty. I was assistant director of nursing for four months while revamping their care plan system. I then went to Long Beach to work in another facility. Again I was assistant director and kept learning things that were necessary for my growth. My eyes were wide open by this time on how some of these facilities were run—most of the time I was horrified. I couldn't work in a facility that didn't take care of its residents. Most owners only cared about the money, but I was determined to make things different once I was in charge. After all, providing top-notch care for our elderly is what it's all about. I lasted at Long Beach for about nine months. These owners' corrupt dealings were not what I was cut out for either—I couldn't stand by and watch what the lack of care did to people. It seemed to me that most of the nursing home owners were corrupt. At that time, Medicare dollars brought in the most money. Owners asked the director of nurses to manipulate facts and figures to improve their bottom line and I could never be a participant in any of those shady dealings.

Then one day, I got a call from Manzo, who offered me the director of nursing position at Montclair, the nursing home he owned. I accepted his offer and stayed at Montclair for four years, enjoying the fruits of my labors like never before. Unfortunately, after four years Manzo sold the facility to the same corrupt owners I had worked for in the past and I knew I couldn't continue with them because of my prior experience, so I left, again.

Next, a friend of mine offered me an assistant position in her facility. It seems like I moved around often, but I was determined to gain all of the knowledge I would need to become a successful director of nursing again. I had proven to myself and others that I was more than up to the task at Manzo's facility. This next facility presented an even higher level of care and acuity. They had a subacute floor with a twelve-bed ventilator unit, which was even farther out of my comfort zone. I learned the entire infection control and in-service regulatory policies and procedures at this location. I had a top-notch director of nursing who taught me how to be the best director I could be. She also taught me how to manage and love the staff. Having staff on your side is the key to running a good facility. I stayed there two and a half years and felt this closed the chapter for me. I now felt competent to go back to being a director and running things my way. The test would soon be upon me. I needed to find a place where I could stay until I retired, which was approximately ten years away. It needed to be one that I could finally mold into my dream care facility and institute policies that would provide our people with the resident-centered, compassionate care they deserved.

It wasn't long before the opportunity came knocking. In 2001 I received a phone call from an administrator of a facility in Woodbury, NY, which was ten minutes from my house. She was recently promoted to be the new administrator and needed someone to replace her as director of nursing. The facility was a two-hundred-bed nursing home. It was the largest I had ever taken on. I felt good about this path and looked forward to seeing where it led and accepted the position.

My philosophy in taking on this new position was to be a compassionate human first, which meant acting as an advocate for the residents and staff. My heart was always primarily with the residents and staff; management came second. I was part of that management structure, but I didn't want to compromise my priority for the sake of someone else's bottom line. Now that I was director of nursing, I had the knowledge and power to make significant changes and to lead in the direction where residents' care and staff concerns were my primary objectives.

I wrote the following journal entries in reference to my experience working in nursing homes and seeing firsthand how they really operate. I had been working in the industry for two years when I began writing.

Journal Entries:

> 8/26/79: As we talk over things and communicate our thoughts to one another, we are able to see things with much more clarity. Talking to you about Forest Glen and a journal was a great idea. It all just really hit me, the dishonesty, greed, selfishness; criticizing, inhuman behavior that goes on is incredible.

> I am trying to be detached, which is usually easy for me, and not allow my emotions to flip me out too much.

The nurses have a tremendous problem with their egos. They all need to be recognized as the "boss." Maybe so do I, but not in the same way.

8/28/79:

Recently the nurses joined forces and voted to join the union, 1199. They were all afraid of losing their jobs, so for security the union seemed like a good idea. We had a few preliminary meetings to air out our many conflicts. Of course the meetings always turned out to be an angry mob getting together. There was a mix of angry nurses and paranoid nurses.

9/7/79:

It's nice to be home where at the moment it's quiet. I have to be able to leave Forest Glen at three o'clock and not take it out the door with me and bring it home.

Forest Glen is in terrible shape and the more I think about it the more convinced I am that the place is being run by the mob, including the administrator.

When doctors order medication for the residents, there is no forethought involved as to the contraindications. I have observed that that's why most of the residents are lethargic. They just sit around and sleep in their chairs or on their beds. Some of them, a small percentage, are active and they participate in life. Those residents are the ones that are less sick and more alert and live a better quality of life. They also take the least amount of medication.

The residents that hardly move are usually full of pain all the time and they are on all sorts of medications for various reasons. Every ailment brings more medications and more side effects. Some of them are on pain medications, laxatives, sleep medications, depression medications, heart medications, rash medications, etc. All taken together. Why?

9/19/79:

Yesterday at work I had to call a doctor to get an order for a resident for cough medication. The doctor I called is known for his abrupt behavior and lack of caring—very typical for doctors in nursing homes to be of that caliber. I informed him the resident is coughing at night and keeping herself and her roommate awake most of the night. This cough is chronic and she just needed some cough suppressant. In an abrupt and quick response he ordered Dalmane, a potent sleeping medication that has many awful side effects. Not great for the elderly who are more sensitive to medications than those in midlife. He also quickly hung up so I was unable to respond back. I wanted to call him back but I didn't. I'm still learning how to navigate my way around and how to stand up for the residents and not feel be intimidated, especially by doctors.

After this episode I called my supervisor to let off steam. She was understanding and told me not to hold on to my anger. I don't believe as nurses we should be humiliated or intimidated by doctors. They are no better or no worse than we are. We are supposed to be a team and work together towards a common goal, the care of each resident. Unfortunately the system doesn't work like that. Most of the doctors are rude and nasty and don't want to be bothered except when they take the residents' money.

The longer I work I see the system failures and it's scary.

When I read my past journal entries and see how I felt back then, I know why I wanted to get my degree and run the nursing home the way I dreamed it should be run. It would be a continuous process of learning.

White Pines was the facility for me. Everything I learned over the last twenty-six years I was able to put into operating a nursing home that's welcoming, loving, and gives good quality care to its residents. I transitioned it into a place where the residents and staff were treated like humans, where the medical team worked together for the best possible outcomes, and where I was able to use my compassion for good and make a tremendous difference.

CHAPTER 11

WHITE PINES: REACHING THE TOP AND MAKING A DIFFERENCE, 2001–2011

White Pines Nursing Home was a unique facility and in spite of its many challenges, the best experience of my professional life. The staff also was the best I have ever worked with. They all had heart, integrity, and a love for the residents. The hurdles were massive as the new director, but with my prior life and professional experiences, I was stronger and more confident to take on a major challenge, and believe me this was it. Here was the opportunity I had waited years for; to create a nursing home with an atmosphere of caring and love.

Mr. and Mrs. Schwartz were the owners of this two-hundred-bed mom-and-pop nursing home. As with most facilities I'd worked for previously, they were your typical nursing home owners; their priority was the bottom line. Jackie was the administrator and had been the director of nursing prior to me taking on the job. The owners paid for her administrator's license, and now she was ready to take on that role at White Pines. Jackie began her relationship with the owners as a nursing assistant many years before. She worked her way up the ladder with financial help from them similarly to the way Manzo helped me climb the ladder. The only difference between Manzo and the Schwartz's was that Manzo had a heart for the patients and staff while for the Schwartz's it was strictly a business, no heart involved.

My gut told me that Jackie and the owners were not honest people and were trying to manipulate me. I had come too far to let anyone take advantage of me. Over the years I had gone from a weak young woman to a savvy professional having acquired the skills necessary to deal with difficult, controlling people. I was not about to let them hijack my plan for a compassionate, resident-centered facility.

Jackie, the administrator, and Drew, the housekeeping supervisor, were in a relationship that was supposed to be a secret—except everyone knew. Because of my past relationships, I could see signs of abuse in their relationship with Drew in total control. I suspected they both were not above stealing from the owners, engaging in shady deals with some of the vendors, and lining their pockets with the kickbacks. I could never find the proof, but it seemed clear that something was going on. Once I began implementing changes, the most vocal resistance, not surprisingly, came from Jackie and Drew. I operate by the book and follow written policy and regulatory guidelines; they clearly were not happy with it. The rest of the staff was wonderful, helpful, and excited to have me there. It was a staff with heart that they demonstrated in the way they cared for the residents. I loved it! I now had strength and professional knowledge. I would need it because my next test was on the way.

Jackie and Drew's longstanding relationship with the owners would be a major hindrance as I sought to turn White Pines into a first-rate nursing home. Because of this close relationship with the owners, Drew would try to intimidate me by talking loudly into my face and invading my personal space. He always gave me a hard time whenever I wanted to implement any changes that would improve the facility and conform to regulations. He would go to Jackie to complain, but because his complaints were about regulatory issues, she knew I was right and had no choice but to take my side.

Living with Dan primed me for dealing with Drew. He was a large African American man, overweight, loud, and obnoxious. He used his massive physicality along with sexual innuendo to try to intimidate me. I simply stood my ground and stared back into his face without blinking. I was the director of nursing and had more power and position than he did. In all other matters, Jackie would back him up, even if he was wrong. To get around Jackie, I simply went to the owners instead. The whole facility was intimidated by him. They would come to me behind his back and complain about him, but they would never face him. He always wanted me to tell him who came to me with a complaint. My answer was, "You'll have to kill me first." I would never betray my staff; my job was to stand up for them when they were right. He was just a bully looking for someone to push around.

One of the first major tasks after I got there was the submission of information to the state about the residents and the care that was needed. This process was called the Patient Review Instrument, or PRI, and was related to the amount of reimbursement from Medicaid the facility would get to care for the residents. Since most of the residents were on Medicaid, that meant a good deal of money for the facility. The process required an audit of the residents' medical records to ensure all the care they are given is correct and documented according to policy and state regulations. At the end there is a score that corresponds to a dollar value. I had done this process many times and knew it well.

Barbara and Cindy were my assistant directors of nursing and what a team we made. Never before had I worked with two such competent and compassionate women in my professional life. I always said, "You couldn't buy us off the shelf." We were a perfect balance to each other. I called us "the holy trinity." We sure needed all the divine intervention we could get.

The three of us together completed the PRI and presented it to Jackie. She immediately said, "That score is too low, we have to raise the score or the owner won't be happy." This wasn't a new response to me as I saw a similar reaction at all of my previous facilities. The bottom line was the most important thing to owners, and they were willing to commit fraud and implicate those under them by asking them to do the same for their bottom line. I was appalled, as were Barbara and Cindy. To bring up the score, the records had to be falsified. My team and I were unwilling to do that and I took a strong stand. We could go to jail and lose our nursing licenses and everything we worked so hard to get. For what? So we could commit fraud on the owner's behalf and steal money for them. The holy trinity decided to make copies of everything that was going to be submitted and continued to do that in the future in order to protect ourselves. The three of us were always on the same page and stood together for ten years. In the end, the holy trinity prevailed.

I continued to not trust Jackie. I knew in order for me to do my job I couldn't let her get in my way. There were some things she told me not to get involved in. A nursing director needs to be involved in everything. One of the things she didn't want me involved in was the residents' diapers. She told me that Drew was in charge and that he had it under control. This made me more suspicious and motivated me to investigate anything she told me to "lay off." The first thing I investigated was the use of diapers. As a nursing director my responsibility was to the residents first. Diapers are a very important issue in nursing. It involves dignity, skin care, and quality of care. I had a vast knowledge of diapers, their cost, and which ones were best for the residents. I needed to know what diaper they were using and how much it was costing. I found out that they were on an automatic delivery every two weeks, whether or not they needed them. It turned out that the facility was paying a huge amount on diapers every month and were using an inferior product. I was able to get the invoices and track it all down. Even though I was told to lay off, I went to the owner and asked him if he liked spending that kind of money per month on diapers. His face dropped and from that moment on he put me in charge of diapers. I ordered a completely different, superior quality diaper at a cheaper price, from a different company and put the delivery at supply and demand. I was able to throw out the crooked supplier Drew was dealing with as well. In order to start the new diapers, I needed to use up what was in house first. It took six months to use up our inventory. Jackie and Drew were not happy with me, but there was nothing they could do. I felt proud to stand up for what was right.

My relationship with Drew continued to deteriorate. I knew he hated me and the feeling was mutual. He would use sexual comments and talk about my body type to try and intimidate me. I was far too strong for him—no longer was I that weak woman from my past. I would look him in the eye and be silent. Then I would follow up with, "Just do it." He finally found a woman he couldn't push around and it drove him crazy.

Something made me go outside my front door one Thanksgiving morning. I walked to my car and was shocked to find a huge stone flower pot—one that had sat in front of my house— smashed into my windshield on the driver's side. My first thought was Drew. While looking at the destruction of the car, I felt this overwhelming wash of anger and hate overtake me—it was coming from the person who threw it. I had no proof Drew was the culprit, but my gut told me it was him. I was horrified and felt violated and threatened. When I went back to work days later, I told the story to Cindy, Barbara, and Jackie. Jackie's first response was, "I'm glad I was out of town." *What a first reaction,* I thought. Her response further convinced me that my initial gut reaction was correct. They did both go out of town, but they left on Thanksgiving evening. The incident occurred Thanksgiving morning.

As time went on Jackie's behavior became erratic and out of control. At some point during this time Jackie and Drew announced they were engaged. It's supposed to be a happy time in a relationship, but I saw a deterioration in her quality of life, and so did the staff that knew her well. She was taking many different medications for different ailments that she claimed she had. She doctor-shopped and was able to get a variety of prescriptions from different doctors. It was easy in our facility to do so because several doctors were in and out every day. She had personal relationships with all of them and they would give her whatever she wanted. It infuriated me, but there was nothing I could do. She called in sick and often left work early, leaving the work of the facility to me, Barbara, and Cindy. This didn't present a problem because the three of us ran that facility like a well-oiled machine. We didn't need Jackie, and at times she was a hindrance to progress and her presence only got in the way of our goals to improve the overall care for the residents. The nursing department wanted and needed to be brought up to higher standards. That was my goal from the beginning of my professional life. To create a more humane treatment for residents and staff and create policies designed to achieve those goals—and we were in the process of doing that at White Pines. The staff was on board to improve care and participate in creating a warm and welcoming atmosphere. Although this staff was wonderful from the beginning they needed strong, caring leadership to support and guide them.

Early one morning, Jackie didn't show up for work. We called her house multiple times to no answer. Barbara and Jackie's sister got in the car and went to her house. Drew was already at work when he heard she was missing. He also got in his car and headed to the house. They found her in her bedroom, dead. It was later reported she had three gunshots to the abdomen. Whether or not they were self-inflicted, no one knew. Of course we were all in a state of shock. The entire facility was mourning. No one wanted it to end this way. Of course all our thoughts turned to Drew having something to do with it. It sounds awful, but it's true. The police investigated and questioned Drew for a number of days. There was no proof of foul play. I always wondered how a person shoots themselves in the abdomen three times. It seemed impossible to me. None of it ever sat right with any of us. The police also questioned the amount of medications she had in her possession. They recognized that she was doctor-shopping. I don't know if anything happened to the doctors, but I think they were questioned as well.

Time went by and the holy trinity was holding the facility together pretty well. At that point Drew was going to retire because he knew how the facility felt about him and everything that went on. He was encouraged by ownership to do so. It took a while, but the facility did recover. We all held on to each other for support and managed to continue to run a great facility. We got a new administrator who was a wonderful man, and we all got along really well. We were able to ascend to a higher level of quality with him at the helm.

New policies and procedures and in-servicing were done to bring up the standards of care in the facility. We were on a roll, doing a great job, and providing good care—having excellent Department of Health inspections and always improving. We had a couple of deficiency-free surveys. The work of the holy trinity and the rest of the staff created a warm, loving, and great care facility. We developed relationships with the residents' families. One family member I was close to was walking by my office while on her phone saying, "Hi, am I talking to Gasper from Sicily?" I freaked out and ran into the hall to ask her to repeat herself. My father was Gasper from Sicily and I guess he was saying hello. That's how I interpreted it. In the end the residents benefitted the most along with the proud staff. They took pride in their work and felt valued. This is how it's supposed to be.

I worked there for ten years and accomplished everything I wanted to in my professional career before retiring in 2011. I gave good care, love, and affection to my residents and staff. I would always visit the dying residents, hold their hands, and let them know they weren't alone and they could let go of this earthly life and soar to heaven.

As I think back on my professional life, I feel a sense of pride knowing that I have touched many lives in a positive way. I also didn't allow any intimidation or control and stood up for my beliefs and the lives of the residents. In the end, my dream of creating a loving nursing home atmosphere that was caring was completed, and in the process I'd become a strong, confident, and empowered woman!

CHAPTER 12

JACKIE AND DREW'S MYSTERIOUS CIRCUMSTANCE: WHAT REALLY HAPPENED?

M any months later I went to my medium, Richard. He was one I'd trusted for many years and he is always right on. Many of my family members have gone to him too. He is the real deal and very specific—no generalities. I wanted to see if I could get some answers about Jackie's death. If anyone could shed some light on this, it would be Richard. When I have a reading it is usually one year apart and I give NO information. I just validate the information he has given me.

As my session with Richard advanced there was a mention of Jackie being there in the beginning of the reading, and that she was off to the side and in the background. Toward the end of my reading I had an opportunity to ask questions. I asked about Jackie. Richard said she was present but was in the background not out in the light. He said she was in the shadows. I expressed my desire to speak to her. He asked if it would be okay if she used some of my energy so she could move into the light. Of course I said yes and she then appeared out in the open to him. Richard's first question to me was, "Who's the bus driver?" Drew had a bus company as a side business for many years. So I knew he was talking about Drew. He then said, "Who was shot in the abdomen?" I freaked and validated the information for him. He hit the nail on the head with such specificity. Richard then said that Drew was indirectly involved in Jackie's death. He said Drew owed a lot of money to very bad people. Richard said that those people were sending a message to Drew to repay the loan. It all made perfect sense to me. Jackie also added that she was sorry about what happened on Thanksgiving morning—again very specific. Richard brought up Thanksgiving—not me! So in death she validated that Drew was the one who threw the flower pot through the car window. For the record, Richard asked very direct questions with specific information. He knew none of the story and I told him nothing.

Cindy, my friend and part of the holy trinity, also went to Richard many months later. He didn't know who we were and only had our first names. There was no connection that Richard knew of between Cindy and me. He told Cindy the exact same thing he told me. So we validated each other.

Months later I was told that Drew had cancer all over his body and was terminal. So within two years of Jackie's death, Drew was dead. Both were too young. Was it karma? Of course it was. It was unfortunate to witness this terrible karmic return.

CHAPTER 13

AUNT DANIELLE'S LIFE FROM 1997–2004: THE FINAL STRAW

By 1997 I was feeling pretty good about my nursing career because I was reaching my goals one step at a time on my way to becoming a director of nursing again— this time armed with the knowledge and experience I needed to succeed at a facility where I could implement resident-centered compassionate care policies. At the same time, I was trying my best to bring my mother's last wish of a cohesive family to fruition. My relationship with my sister was on a steady decline. Caring for my beloved Aunt Danielle seemed a step in the right direction toward bridging the chasm that existed in the family. Aunt Danielle was growing older and I felt confident that as an RN I had the expertise to provide the additional care she now needed.

Aunt Danielle was my mother's younger sister. Both of my mother's sisters have left a huge and positive impact on the lives of me and my children. Aunt Danielle was the last remaining sister. She was a stunning woman; well put together and stylish. She had been a model in her younger years and demonstrated it in the way she put together her outfits with matching hats, gloves, and shoes. She was a girly girl. Aunt Danielle never married. She was an independent woman who never had to rely on a man and over the years, due to her business savvy, she managed to amass quite a healthy sum of money.

During this time, Aunt Bea, my mom's middle sister, was near death in a nursing home when Aunt Danielle fell and fractured her hip. The only people they had were me and Tom and the kids. My brother was nowhere to be found—he was always hiding somewhere, and my sister was in New Jersey with Uncle-Daddy, where she would spew negative comments, after the fact, on what we did or didn't do, but was otherwise unavailable when a crisis was actually happening. My husband and I went into Brooklyn to be with Aunt Danielle and help her get through whatever was going to cross her path.

Danielle needed surgery and had to go to a rehabilitation facility for physical therapy. It just so happened that's my business! I knew a lot of people and had connections in the healthcare industry. If Tom and I were going to be Danielle's caregivers, it was important for me to gather her finances, secure a power of attorney, and become authorized as her health care agent. Tony Manzo, my mentor, advised me to hire an attorney to have the needed paperwork drawn up and signed. We got a lawyer to complete all the necessary paperwork while she was still sharp as a tack. I knew she had quite a bit of stocks and bonds and hidden money and needed someone to help her. This was all done while she was clearly of sound mind. No one ever knew how much she really had. I only knew that I had to preserve it in order for her to have enough to continue to financially take care of her needs. At this time she was eighty-one. Going through surgery at her age was not easy physically or mentally. Bea being on her deathbed only magnified an already complex issue. All this took money and I knew she had the means; I just had to gather it all and organize everything. Danielle told me where she had the stock certificates and treasury bonds and how to access them and her safe deposit box. She filled Tom and me in on everything including payments to Aunt Bea's nursing home, which she was paying privately every month. We put her assets in a brokerage house not connected to the family. This was an important step to avoid family disputes. It was always about preserving her assets for her care and needs, not for the family to confiscate and do with it what they thought was right. My brother and sister, however, had a different opinion.

Aunt Bea died while Danielle was in the hospital and there was nothing she could do. Tom and I handled the funeral arrangements. Having her power of attorney allowed me to arrange the funeral without a problem. I bought a crypt with room for two in the same mausoleum my mother was in so they could be close. When it was Danielle's time she would be placed with her sister. The crypt cost ten thousand dollars; Danielle had the extra funds and I wanted them to have a beautiful spot together forever near my mother.

My brother and sister came to Bea's funeral but no help was offered and I didn't expect it. At this point they weren't sure how much money was involved but they seemed to think I was taking advantage of Danielle.

I learned at one point, my brother had borrowed ten thousand dollars from Danielle to invest. Greg was an independent stockbroker, working on Wall Street at the time. He signed a promissory note to her. Danielle told me all this while she was in my care. Over the years I remember my father saying, "I lost all my money." Apparently Greg also borrowed from my father. Danielle told me Greg was supposed to pay her back monthly. He paid back only a small fraction and never paid back what he owed and she was not happy about it. With that history, Danielle knew she couldn't trust Greg.

Danielle also felt that Maggie could not be trusted. The way she played with my support money showed her intentions were questionable. It was because of my siblings' reputation and my nursing experience and connections that Aunt Danielle made the decision to allow Tom and me to handle her business.

Tom and I took responsibility for cleaning out Danielle's apartment and getting her finances in order. We also had to pay her current bills so we needed to go through the apartment piece by piece to find missing financial items. At Aunt Danielle's behest, I kept Maggie and Greg out of everything because they showed no interest except when there was money involved.

Cleaning Danielle's apartment was a difficult task because she was a hoarder. Maggie asked if she could help with the apartment. I told her how overwhelming it was and appreciated the help. She went once and freaked out after seeing how much work was involved. She took what she wanted and left the rest for the landlord to do. Taking what you want and leaving the rest for the landlord wasn't right, but Maggie told me it was just too much work and she wasn't going to do it anymore.

Danielle needed to redo her will because her original had Vera as her executor—but now Vera was deceased. She had her lawyer redo the will making me her executor and Tom co-executor. When deciding how to distribute her wealth, I begged her to divide it up equally among Greg, Maggie, and myself. I knew there would be hell to pay if it wasn't. I already knew that my two siblings thought I was unduly influencing Danielle and would make my life a living hell if she didn't. But Danielle was a very stubborn woman and she insisted that I get sixty percent, Maggie get thirty percent, and Greg get nothing. She was still so furious at Greg for not paying her back the ten thousand dollars. It was an ongoing theme. The other ten percent would go to her brother, if he was still alive. Tom talked her into letting Greg have Danielle's brother's ten percent, if he was deceased. She told me she wanted to divide the money up according to who she felt deserved it and who helped her the most. That's the way she thought and no one could change her mind. She did finally agree to give Greg her brother's share if he was deceased.

After Danielle's surgery, we moved her into a rehabilitation facility in Roslyn, NY. I knew the administrator and the staff pretty well and was confident she would get great care there. After utilizing all her allowable Medicare days, we moved her into my facility, White Pines, so that I could keep a close watch on her and be involved in her care. This way I could give her what she needed with our loving caregivers. She recuperated very well for her age. She was up on her feet walking using a walker at first then a cane. Eventually she didn't need any assistive devices. She spent a few weeks at White Pines before she was ready to be independent. She wanted her own place and we felt it was best if we looked into assisted living facilities. She would have independence and also supervision. She moved into our house until we could find her a nice facility. She spent six months with us while we looked at facilities. It was a difficult time because she took over the house and became the center of our attention. We got through it and found her a beautiful assisted living facility in Huntington, NY. She loved it there and made many friends, which she needed. I knew all the doctors in the area and set her up with one of them so she could be followed with care. I took her back and forth to her doctor visits and kept up on her medical needs.

She did well for seven years and had a good quality of life. She loved the facility and was able to leave and go shopping in the area. On holidays we would pick her up and include her and her boyfriend, Josh. I had spent every holiday of my life with Danielle and Josh; the holidays just wouldn't have been the same without them.

Danielle started to go downhill fast seven years after her hip surgery. She was eighty-eight at the time. She started to get dementia, needed to wear diapers, and was unable to feed herself. She now required round the clock care. The facility she was in had a home care agency connected to it so we were able to get her the care she needed without moving her. The agency was going to make sure she had consistent caregivers because I knew this was very important, especially with dementia patients. Her care costs ran about fifteen thousand a month. That was cash money coming out of her account. It was a good thing we preserved her money because her funds were what had been paying for her care until now. The assisted living facility was also paid privately from her account. I knew she had enough money for her care until she passed—for that I was grateful. It was important to bring all her financials together for her benefit, not mine, Maggie's, or Greg's. I remember Maggie saying to me early on when we were looking at facilities, why don't you put her in a home in Connecticut. I asked her why Connecticut where she knows no one and we are so far away. "It's cheaper," she said. I didn't listen to any of her suggestions because I didn't see where they benefited Aunt Danielle. It should also be noted that up until now there had been no communication with my siblings regarding Aunt Danielle's care.

While all of this was taking place, my sister was working on poisoning my daughter Lisa's mind against me. It was getting close to the end for Danielle and Maggie knew there was money involved and became more interested. The way I saw it, Maggie felt she had no control over me anymore so she would use Lisa to get to me. Lisa and I at times have had a strained relationship and Maggie was going to exploit it to control me—or so she thought.

Maggie began to tell Lisa that Danielle was getting shoddy care. She couldn't possibly know because in the past seven years she had never come to visit her—even when she was dying. Because Danielle was close to death she was not eating or drinking enough to sustain life. This is what happens at the end of life. The body doesn't require food. I have worked long enough in nursing homes to recognize the signs. As an RN, I knew better than anyone how to care for a dying patient—especially someone as dear to me as my Aunt Danielle. Lisa was vulnerable at the time and began to believe the lies Maggie was spewing. Neither one knew how to care for someone at the end of life. I was Danielle's health care agent and she told me when she was lucid how she wanted the end of her life to be. This is a very important conversation to have. She told me she didn't want any feeding tubes or any other lifesaving procedures. She wanted to go with dignity when it was time. We discussed things in complete detail. I told her I would honor her wishes.

The time came when Danielle was close to death and she was having a lot of difficulty breathing. The facility didn't have oxygen to give her and knowing that oxygen is a comfort measure, I called my dear friend Cindy, a nurse, for some advice. We discussed sending her to the hospital to make her more comfortable. I spoke with her doctor as well and we decided to send her. Not for life sustaining measures; only for comfort. I felt I wasn't going against her wishes. I did verbalize it to Danielle but I don't know if she really understood. While all this was going on, my sister called me yelling and shrieking that I needed to send Danielle to the hospital and get a feeding tube put in her and that I was starving her to death. I ignored her, hung up, and decided to send her to the hospital for comfort measures. I'm sure Maggie thought she bullied me into doing so and that's why I sent her. We got to the hospital and a few hours later she passed quietly and comfortably.

We made funeral arrangements; she would be buried with her sister Vera, in the same crypt in a beautiful mausoleum room around the corner from my mother. I wanted them all to be together. In life they lived in a not so nice neighborhood, so in death I wanted to step it up a little.

It was now the night of Danielle's wake and many friends and family showed up. Maggie, Dan, Lisa, and her husband, Chris, came together. They completely ignored me and never spoke to me the entire night. The negativity in the room was palpable. It was so thick that everyone was commenting on it. I felt Maggie was trying to intimidate me but I wasn't having it. I just stayed away from all of them. My brother, Greg, came to the wake alone. He too spoke very little. He told me that he wouldn't be at the funeral but his wife would attend. At some point he said to me, "If I was in charge of the money I would have divided it equally in three parts, not different amounts to each." The stipulation in Danielle's will was that Greg got nothing and that the final ten percent went to her brother. She added if he was deceased then Greg would get the ten percent. At that time he was deceased. I figured while I had them now, at the funeral, I would ask about his death certificate in order to release Greg's money. Greg and his wife were his executors so they had access to the document and I thought my sister-in-law could bring it to the funeral. This had nothing to do with my inheritance or Maggie's, only Greg's. Somehow when my sister-in-law delivered the message to Maggie and Lisa, I was now a "money hungry bitch who has some nerve discussing money on the day of the funeral." I was again the bad guy and only in it for the money. My question was *where were any of you in the last eight years?* My thinking was it would make it easier for Greg but it didn't work out that way and frankly I didn't care what any of them thought of me after the fact. Danielle and I know the truth.

The day of the funeral, I was presented with Danielle's brother's death certificate and otherwise had no conversation with any of them. After the burial, as a group we walked over to visit my mother's crypt. At some point someone said, "Let's go to Nanu's grave" (my father). We all thought it was a good idea. My father was buried in the ground across the street in keeping with his Italian heritage. I always had a hard time finding his grave so I went into the office and got the number for his spot. It was still difficult to find. We all got out of cars and were wandering around looking. There were about fifteen of us. None of us could find it. Lisa was parallel to me and said in a very nasty tone, "Maybe if you came more often you would remember where it is." She was about thirty feet away from me. My response to her was, "And maybe if you came more often you too would know where it was." The look she gave me was that of her father, Dan. She began to run toward me like she was going to attack me or more. I remember that look very well. All I saw was Dan coming at me and I reverted back to the past. This action triggered my PTSD and at that moment it came to the surface. I turned and walked back to the group with her on my heels, ready to pounce. I felt the tension in the air and was overwhelmed with fear—that fear that I get deep down inside. I got to the group and my other children, Tee, Kelly, Casey, Seth, and Ryan, all protected me. They created a physical barrier to keep Lisa from getting to me. I don't even remember what was said; I only remember it being a screaming match. My sister was at her car watching the entire, seemingly planned scenario play out the way she wanted. My sister-in-law and my grandson, Joe, was also present and watching along with her. She must have been in her glory. This is what she lives for, to see me suffer and be in pain, especially at the hands of my daughter. They all got in their car and drove away like a bat out of hell, tires screeching and leaving dust.

After the hostile group left and things calmed down, we found my father's grave. It was right in front of our eyes. I'm sure Nanu didn't approve of their behavior and blocked his grave from view. The remaining family all held hands and danced and sang joyfully around his grave. We ended the day by going out to eat.

It was a rough few days. As soon as I got home I got a phone call from Maggie. She demanded to know how much money was in the estate and wanted the lawyer's number. (I thought we were money hungry if we talked about money on the day of the funeral. I guess that rule only applies to me.) I gave her the information; she had a right to know because she was named in the will. Of course the conversation was screaming and yelling. I could hear her son in the background also carrying on and screaming.

Maggie called the lawyer and then called me back again saying that it was impossible for Danielle to assign Tom to be co-executor. She was furious and continued to yell. I just hung up on her. I did that often because there was no way of having a civil conversation with her screaming at me. She had told the lawyer that Danielle was afraid of Tom and thought he might try to murder her. Can you even imagine such a thing? Danielle certainly never told me that and she was one to always speak her mind. Danielle knew Tom was with me every step of the way. Maggie lived in New Jersey and she never saw her, so Danielle felt Tom was the better choice for her needs. I didn't hold a gun to her head. This idea was all hers. No one could tell her any different. She was a woman of her own mind and the whole family was well aware of that.

By the end of the day I was in full-blown PTSD mode. I thought Maggie was going to send Dan to murder me. If I heard noise I would jump up and look at the window waiting for the devil to show up. My body and mind were saturated with fear and anxiety. I had been going to a therapist, and was in desperate need of seeing one now. It was rough for a while living in fear of bad things happening. Eventually it passed with time—as it usually does—until the next trigger.

Lisa and the entire family didn't speak for eighteen months. It was a very long, difficult time.

After eighteen months passed we all began speaking again. It was wonderful! We found out that at the time of Danielle's death, Lisa was pregnant and in the process of a miscarriage at Danielle's funeral. No wonder she was so vulnerable. Maggie and her whole fiasco created an atmosphere of hate and darkness in my daughter and son-in-law's life and home. Maggie brought negative, dark energy into the house with her and used her darkness to poison my daughter and her husband. In the process, Lisa and Chris lost a baby. Chris relayed to me later that Maggie and her son were all screaming to each other about the money and how they thought it wasn't fair that I got sixty percent and Maggie got thirty percent.

As for Greg, he got his ten percent share minus the ten thousand he owed Danielle. Tom and I found the original promissory note in her apartment that was signed by him. We gave it to the lawyer and at least in death she was paid back and he didn't get away with it. It sure felt good because I knew how upset Danielle was.

Finally, I had reached my limit. After all that had taken place, I made the difficult decision to remove Maggie and Dan and Greg permanently from of my life. I had tried my best to fulfill my mother's wish, but this experience showed me the impossibility of the task. Not only had I not managed to bring the family together, but it resulted in me being estranged from my daughter Lisa. Now that we were reunited, I was not about to let it happen again!

CHAPTER 14

THE RECKONING: A TIME TO LET GO

A deathbed letter from your mother is one of those things you don't expect that affects you on a visceral level. My mother was on her deathbed when she wrote it to me in 1978 as I was trying to come to terms with her terminal diagnosis from colon cancer, yet I knew it came from her heart. I had stored the letter away in a box after reading it and never touched it again because it was too painful. It caused bewilderment, anxiety, guilt, and anger, and although I never read it again, it influenced my life for many years to come. Why did I allow it to do so? Although she didn't provide me with much guidance growing up, she was a loving mother and we were close. I was her confidante and I loved her dearly. So, in pursuit of my mother's request for me to reunite the family, I would spend the next twenty-five years seeking to fulfill her dream and although I never accomplished it, I don't regret trying. In the end, instead of reuniting the family, we are now estranged.

I often wondered, given my history of poor choices, lack of self-esteem, and ability to control my own life as a young woman, why my mother thought I was, as she wrote, "the strong one." I certainly didn't reveal strength in my actions at the time—I was weak and controlled—and she knew about all of it. After much consideration, I came to the conclusion that what she defined as "the strong one" was actually "the empathetic one." Compassion was and still is one of my strongest traits and what guided me as I rose through the ranks in my professional life. I think my mother knew her children and understood that I was the only sibling who would at least give it a try—and I did! It took a huge chunk of my life. After the fiasco at Aunt Danielle's funeral, I realized one person can only do so much—it requires cooperation between all parties to effect a change of heart. While trying to do right by my family, not only did I fail in that regard, but I nearly lost my daughter Lisa in the process. At this point, the futility of my twenty-five-year effort became clear and I began to reconsider what had turned into an empty pursuit.

It was 2005, I was still living in New York, and on this particular day I was home alone in my bedroom. Something made me reach into the wooden box where my mother's letter had been stored undisturbed for decades. I remove it with purpose from its case and hold it up and read it one final time. After I finish reading, I clutch it for a few more minutes trying to connect with my mother's spirit and recall all that had happened in my life that had caused her to write this letter in the first place. I feel warmth wash over me and begin to sense my mother's presence. I am at peace. The thoughts that enter into my mind are Mom, I have honored you all these years; *I love you and I know you meant well, but this burden to unite our family is too difficult for one person to achieve. I've spent the better part of my life pursuing your dream to no avail. I'm fifty-eight years old now and the children are grown with lives of their own. What more can I do! Isn't it time to free me from this burden and allow me to spend my remaining years in peace?*

At this point, without hesitation, I reach for the lighter, hold the letter up, and light the paper's edge. As the flame ignites, I see a stream of smoke rise, sense the cleansing power of the fire, and with it a burning away of all of the negative elements from my past, until all that is left of the letter is a small heap of grayish ash—and it is done.

I pray the Phoenix will rise from these ashes and the fire that signifies death and rebirth will transform from the old, a new and glorious future free of guilt, anger, and anguish!

CHAPTER 15

RETIRING TO SMALL TOWN USA: HENDERSONVILLE, NORTH CAROLINA

The first few years were difficult. Retiring and moving out of state are life changing. Leaving the kids and the grandkids behind was upsetting and a struggle for me. I knew I would go back to New York often and for special occasions to see them. I knew they were not very happy with our plans either. I totally get it. They were angry and blamed the move on Tom, believing he was the one that was influencing me. Nothing could be farther from the truth. Tom and I were both on the same page regarding the move. I was very willing and didn't need to be forced into anything. I was not that weak woman anymore. I don't think the kids believed, at that time, that I was strong and not so easy to manipulate into moving if I didn't want to go. Tom and I felt their anger and just allowed them to feel what they were feeling. It eventually subsided on its own.

Our son Ryan made the move with us because he really needed to get out of New York and start fresh somewhere else. It was the best move he made and I felt redeemed knowing that we had a hand in making the move possible. I always felt it was one of the reasons we had to move — to save Ryan. We did!

We had other valid reasons for leaving New York. The cost of everything in New York is astronomical. We were going to be on a limited income and the weather was also a factor. We needed a warmer climate without harsh winters. My body is full of arthritis and the cold, damp, snowy weather is not good for me. I felt it would add years onto my life going to a less severe climate.

Once in North Carolina, I had a lot of guilt leaving the kids. The family dynamics fell apart and my PTSD kicked in. Tom and I were fighting a lot and we were not in a good place. I stayed in PTSD for about two years. It was awful. I kept it all inside. I was fearful of resorting to old habits; I started looking over my shoulder, expecting Dan to appear with murderous intentions. Tom's anxiety increased and so did his blood pressure. We finally got it together and things calmed down, but it was a rough period.

Clearly I needed to get back into some form of therapy to help me. I had to get to the bottom of all of it. Asheville was the perfect place for me, as it was a larger version of Port Washington—full of my kind of people. Asheville is a city in the Blue Ridge Mountains, known for its art scene and historic architecture. That's where I continued my healing journey, through unconventional therapies. I'd been down the traditional therapy road and now I needed something different, something deeper. I'm most comfortable and open to different types of therapies.

Asheville is a hippie, new age community with all kinds of new age healing options. This was right up my alley and I had a new path to get to the real hidden bullshit that has been hiding inside of me far too long. I didn't want to live the rest of my life without getting to the bottom of why I put myself into destructive relationships and why I tolerated them as long as I did. I also had a great need to get rid of the pain, shame, guilt, regret, self-loathing, and many other negative feelings that I carried around every day—not only for me but for my children and my relationships. I was also of the belief that if I didn't face it head on I would have to carry it around with me from life to life. First I had to find out the details in order to face it.

CHAPTER 16

SEEKING PROFESSIONAL THERAPY: MY HEALING JOURNEY BEGINS!

Therapy/Shredding and Forgiving

I was fifty-four when I began my healing journey in 2001. It took me this long to reach out for therapy. I had so much buried deep inside of me that I knew needed to be straightened out or I was going to live the rest of my life with these awful feelings about myself, suffer from PTSD, and remain in constant physical pain. I needed to get to the bottom of my life and my relationship with my sister.

My first therapist was Joan. She was a certified social worker who had her own private practice. Joan took me through traditional therapy which opened my mind and put my thoughts in order so I could see them clearly. I loved and adored her and she began my road to healing, forgiving, and loving me. Joan made me aware that I had PTSD. Knowing that opened up my awareness to a whole new level. It made me realize why I was the way I was and why I reacted to situations in a certain way. I was always curious about my early childhood as well because I had no memory of much of it. I was also curious as to why I picked two such awful men and why I chose to go through the situations I placed myself into. In therapy, these were the issues that we addressed in order to provide clarity and to fully understand my past and make changes accordingly. It begins with self-awareness.

During this traditional psychotherapy with Joan it was revealed that my sister was my early childhood abuser. That was a lot to take in but it did make perfect sense. That was as far as it got but I learned so much from that type of therapy that it started me on my road to healing. I was beginning to form a strong foundation toward my self-discovery. These are the issues I learned from traditional therapy:

I have PTSD and it does creep into my life from time to time. My question was, when did this start, and what brought it on initially? Therapy revealed that I had been abused in early childhood by my older sister. I remained in therapy until we moved to North Carolina.

It was in North Carolina that I moved from traditional therapy to alternative therapy. My reasoning was to go deeper by using all of the available methods to bring closure to the emotional baggage I had been carrying for so many years.

These are the therapies I tried in the order that I sought them out:

Astrology/ Past Life Regression:

My first stop on my journey was to an astrologer and a past life regression therapist. Both were fascinating and the message was that I had been controlled and abused starting in early childhood. I have been getting that message from every reading I have gone to since I was a young girl. There is always a message of early childhood abuse. My problem is I don't remember any of it. When I got my palm read, there was the same message; "early childhood trauma" appeared. During the regression, I was also in meditation, and I saw a relationship between husband and wife and child. I was asked to look at my feet and I saw bear feet on rocks. It looked like ancient times. The husband was very abusive and controlling and the woman was submissive. The husband in that life was my sister in this life and we are returning to this life together to work that karma out. The child in that life was my daughter Kelly in this life.

So now I was aware and validated that some nightmare occurred with my sister, only I had no idea what. I had to continue on this road until I found the answers. Each therapist led me to the next therapist. That's how I chose my path. I had full trust and faith that they would lead me in the right direction.

Somatic Therapy:

My next stop was a somatic therapist. Somatic therapy is an alternative medicine. It is used for healing abuse, amongst other things. Somatic therapy incorporates mind, body, spirit, and emotions in the healing process. It has also been explained to me that when abuse occurs at a young age, before language, the abuse memory remains in the body and is stored in our muscles and fascia. It happens this way because the child had no language to describe what was happening. Through guided meditation you can regain that memory. According to therapists, the trauma is trapped within the body and reflected in your body language. Their belief is that all repressed emotions are reflected in your personality, muscle tension, posture, and physical movement. It is called "body armor." I have had posture issues, muscle soreness and tightness, and back pain my entire life. I also discovered I had scoliosis and arthritis, which added to the problem.

On my visits with my therapist, she took me through meditations and each session left me emotionally drained and crying, but in a good way. Not knowing about the body armor at that time, I had a session where I saw myself wearing armor across my chest. It was beautiful to me and it also had shoulder protection too. There was an angel on the front chest plate. This was what I built for myself for protection against the abuse. During this session I was able to take it off and describe it. It felt good to be relieved of it. I have always felt heavy on my shoulders and back and carried myself pitching forward. This all made sense! I later learned that I was protecting my heart. Still not knowing the details, I knew that I was opening up.

During another session, I was taken to a cloud prior to birth into this life. I was told that the cloud was going to take me to my next life (which was this present life). While I was on this cloud I burst into tears and I started shaking uncontrollably. I was saying, "No, I can't go in that house." I couldn't control myself. My somatic therapist asked what I wanted to do. I told her I didn't want to go into that house and I wanted to stay on the cloud, which is what I did and I began to calm down. The physical reaction was huge and undeniable. Why was my reaction so real and deep? In the past whenever I was really scared an odd feeling of dread deep in the center of my chest came upon me. It was very uncomfortable and I knew danger was nearby. That was the feeling that took over me while on that cloud going into my present life. It was a feeling of dread deep within my soul and my being. Why was my emotion so high? Because my spirit knew what was going to happen to me when I was born into my next life and I was afraid. Those feelings were so real that I had to take it to the next level and find out about that house and face what was waiting for me there.

So through these somatic sessions I was able to confirm that it was Maggie, my sister, who was my abuser in my early childhood. My first (traditional) therapist told me the same thing. Every time Maggie was manifested during meditation my body started shaking and that deep chest discomfort occurred which I knew meant fear and danger. I learned that touch for me was a message of danger. That too made sense. I never thought it would be Maggie, and in the beginning I didn't want to believe it; yet, it all made sense.

During my therapy sessions, my somatic therapist helped me fill in a large gap in my memory and I will always be grateful to her for helping me to unlock one of the mysteries of my past. Now I could continue on my road with a little more information to help me put the pieces together.

Medium:

A medium was the next stop on my path, August 2014, to see if I could reach my parents and uncover whether they were aware of my sister's abuse. I had gone to mediums many times, starting as a young woman, so I am able to identify whether or not they are the real deal. I am a believer in mediums and that's because they have proven to me that they are speaking to the other side. I always get detailed readings which provide resolution and peace. I have found that whenever a reading has a lot of detail that only you know, it has the potential to blow your mind.

I went to a medium in Asheville. For some reason I was attracted to finding my healing there. The medium did reach my parents. My mother was a lot more vocal, and my father called me "baby," which is what he called me when he was alive. They both always show up when I need them. They give me signs when I ask for them, so it validates their presence. For instance, if I am in the car and need my mother, I ask her to give me a sign that she's there. Not long after my request, her song would come on the radio. Lou Rawls's "You'll Never Find another Love Like Mine." That was the song she danced to naked every morning for two hours. That's validation for me. I receive many validations and that's because I pay attention to the universe.

My parents told me that they had no idea that Maggie was abusing me when they were alive. My mother said that from her position now she can see the abuse that my sister inflicted on me. She said it occurred from a young age, in the crib. She went on to say that my sister wasn't prepared to be reborn into this current life and was fighting it. She had karmic issues related to black magic that she didn't want to deal with. During her birth, she continued, her soul split in half. Half came into this present life and half stayed in the other dimension. My mother also said that she has a chemical imbalance in combination with the soul split which manifests as a psychopathic personality disorder. I was told to feel sorry for her and pray for her. I was also told that my karma with her is over in this life. It has been dealt with and can be released. They also told me they were sorry and were proud of me as a parent, in spite of all the odds against me. My parents apologized again and left me with a message that I must go on a healing journey and I needed to start now and get through it by the fall equinox. You see, for me that made perfect sense because I follow astrology and knew that it was always good to follow planetary recommendations. So I continued my journey. From here it was recommended that I go to someone for soul retrieval and DNA cleaning. Trauma causes the soul to split. We leave our consciousness in order to protect ourselves and to avoid the full impact of the pain. Soul retrieval has been around for thousands of years. Shamans are the vehicle to perform the retrieval.

My Shaman, Raven:

Soul retrieval is an important level in spiritual healing. It's a process which mends the fragmented self. The effects of trauma cause parts of the soul to leave the body. This process occurs in order to survive the experience by escaping its full impact. Some symptoms associated with soul loss are depression, PTSD, suicidal ideations, and addiction. The shaman moves into an altered state of consciousness to other hidden spirit worlds to retrieve the parts. I know it sounds crazy to some people, but not to me. We have a spiritual body that gets sick too. In order to heal, our entire body needs attention. Traditional Western medicine pays no attention to our spiritual selves, only to our physical bodies, and it treats us with medications and vaccines that have side effects. Why not incorporate the two, traditional and alternative, and be an active participant?

Shamanism is one of the oldest spiritual practices. Shamans have always been leaders in their communities, healing the injured and sick, performing ceremonies, singing, chanting, and dancing. They are the bridge between the living and the dead.

I entered my next step on my healing journey by searching for a shaman. My method of finding a therapist was to google what I'm looking for, read bios, view pictures, and request recommendations from the therapists that have helped me so far. I pick the one that appeals to me the most and the one that my gut tells me is right. I always have luck making decisions that way.

I found my shaman and her name is Raven. Raven is a shamanic priestess who is also a counselor. She has changed my life and made me aware of the whole ugly mess of who I was and who I am now. She has helped me with my memory issues and she also made me realize how important forgiveness is. I realized that I needed to go through whatever it is I went through in the past, like all humans have to, in order for the Phoenix to rise out of the ashes. To be the best you can be without all the restrictions of the past. That's what I want for my life now.

My Shamanic Journey: 9/2/14

My first session with Raven was a shamanic journey. Below is the synopsis of my journey.

Nancy's Journey 9-2-14 (As documented by her Shaman, Raven)

> I called in your spirit guides to direct your journey and was met by several ancestors, including your parents and an angelic being who is with you always. I was taken through several lifetimes and back to the medieval period when I found your body in a lying position. I called in your spirit doctors to address any areas of concern.

> They began clearing energetic debris from your body, work you have done, but the residue was still there. I saw gray sand-like material flowing out. They showed me that you had 32 black cords attached. These represent shame and/or guilt, either on your part or the person to whom they are attached at the other end. Some related to your second husband. They were all cut and dissolved into light. These are big energy drainers, so you may feel new reserves in a few days.

I was told that you needed a soul retrieval of 11 parts that had been either broken off in trauma or given away freely to others. Your spirit guides retrieved these and placed them in your solar plexus. However, I was told that you needed to actively participate, which prompted the ceremony after.

Your sister had severe karma with the lineage you were born into from some intense black magic lifetimes ago. She refused to deal with it for several more lifetimes, but was almost forced to come in this time to take care of it. She didn't want to and half of her broke off before entering the body; so she is basically a half-soul, leaving her open to all kinds of attachments and issues.

This family you were born into was not your lineage, but you made the decision to come in and take care of this unbalanced karma that she (and others) had made. You came to balance the karma for this soul group and you have mostly done that. Yay for you!

Your third husband is in YOUR soul group and came to help you complete your mission. Next your spirit guides began to dissolve your body. I saw the skin melt off and into the earth, then the muscles, organs, bones. It was alarming, and when I asked what was going on, you began to be rebuilt from the earth. I was told that your DNA was being reprogrammed and the story in your cells being rewritten. The story they were giving you is:

"I am whole. I am healthy, my relationships are loving. The world is my temple, all acts are sacred, all life is ceremony." Put this mantra where you can see it and continue to say it, breathing it into every cell of your body. It is like food for you because it is the very coding of your cellular makeup now.

I saw your son Seth with a lot of darkness around him—denoting depression, lack of purpose, not doing his sacred work. He had some attached entities and I cleared him, but they soon came back. He needs to learn to clear himself and know that his thoughts, words, and deeds are creating his life. This will take a big shift for him. He came to heal for his paternal line. I'm happy to talk to him if you can get him to call.

This is a time for you, Nancy, to enjoy life and all the beauty in every day. As you learn to love yourself, your relationship with your dear husband will deepen. You have come into this life shouldering karma for an entire soul group and you have mostly balanced it. You raised 6 children and are with your soulmate. Be proud of what you have accomplished because you are a rock star! A mantra your guides gave me is "I am a beautiful, light-filled expression of the Divine. As I heal, all are healed."

At the end of your journey, a deer showed up as a spirit animal. Deer's message is that you are highly sensitive and gentle in your approach. The deer totem wisdom imparts those with a special connection with this animal with the ability to be vigilant, move quickly, and trust their instincts to get out of the trickiest situations.

The meaning associated with the deer combines both soft, gentle qualities with strength and determination:

- Gentleness

- Ability to move through life and obstacles with grace

- Being in touch with inner child, innocence

- Being sensitive and intuitive

- Vigilance, ability to change directions quickly

- Magical ability to regenerate, being in touch with life's mysteries

Overall: This was a clearing and healing journey and a lot of work was done. We have a tendency to reject this kind of work, especially soul retrievals. Please don't! Keep your energy drawn in for a few days; nurture yourself as if you have brought home a new baby because indeed you have! Drink lots of water and each night place your hand on your solar plexus and welcome these new parts home. Own the work that was done on all levels. If memories or emotions come up, just let them pass on through. No need to process, the work has already been completed.

It sometimes takes up to 3 days to experience in the physical what has been done in the ethereal. Sometimes it is instantaneous.

It was an honor to journey with you, Nancy! Thank you for trusting me in this process on your path.

Much love to you,

Raven

After the session I felt great! I felt lighter! I felt I could now explore the horror that was inflicted on me and my children with a more open mind. I felt strong enough now to delve into the details of my journey so far. I knew I would eventually need to get to the forgiveness part and that it would be very difficult. I began sessions on a regular basis with Raven in order to get to a better place, achieve awareness and forgiveness and finally freedom from the past.

12/30/14: I began my sessions with Raven. Our first session was to set goals for myself. I realized that I have a lot of work to do if I am going to live the rest of my life in peace, health, and happiness. It's a tall order! I also realized that I need to do this on my own without any interference from anyone. I got here alone and alone is the way forward. It is a solitary journey. I do realize that I would not be the person I am today without all my experiences, good and bad; therefore, I wouldn't change anything because I am a now a strong, independent woman and my experiences were what made me that way. I am finally seeing the amazing person I really am. Up to this point I'd never said that—ever. I know that my soul agreed to this life with all its lessons prior to my birth. All lessons are for one purpose—soul evolution. For me this means that God created us in his image. In order to get there we must experience it all. We need many lives in order to accomplish this. Only then will we reach perfection and be Godlike. I realized that I needed this life in this way, in order for me to grow and learn. As hurtful as it was I realize this was the way it needed to be. So forgiveness should be easy, right? We'll see.

As part of my journey with Raven, I needed to write my story then and now. This is what I wrote.

2/20/15: Old Story:

My old story is about a woman, me, who was

- fearful

- cheated on

- controlled

- lived life to only survive, unhappy, abused physically, emotionally, sexually, and spiritually and allowed it

- was sad

- was way too fertile, always pregnant, which led to five abortions; lots of guilt related to that also allowed it

- was totally repressed somewhere deep inside myself

- had a poor self-image

- was dependent and naive

- carried guilt, regret, shame related to my children and the situations I put them in

New Story:

- I am no longer that person. I am no longer fearful every day, looking out windows to make sure no one is coming to murder me or harm me. I have come a long way in the fear category. I live a life of monogamy. I am a much happier person with much to be thankful for, especially my family.

- My fertile days are over, thank God, but I will always cherish the children I brought into this world and in my other lives. I also cherish the souls of the ones that were aborted. I realize that they were never meant to be born. I know they are there watching over me. I no longer live in a naive world. I am well aware of the world around me and I can see how my participation in it has helped many people. I know my goodness and can now see how smart I really am.

- I am beautiful.

- I will never allow anyone to abuse or control me anymore and will only be with someone who allows me to be free. That's Tom! He knows I have to be my own person and understands that's my lesson in this life. I will only depend on myself and I do not need to be dependent on anyone. I can take care of myself in all aspects of life, including financially. One of my big life lessons was to be independent, self-sufficient, and never to be in a situation where someone is ruling my life and abusing me and my children because I have no way out and no means to take care of my family on my own. This is one big lesson I want to pass on to my daughters and sons. It is of utmost importance especially for women to make sure they are independent and self-sufficient. It's the most important lesson.

5/26/15:

During one of my sessions with Raven, she had a vision of a letter that I left for Dan when we escaped. The letter said I was leaving for good and won't be coming back. I knew he would freak out and start looking for me and the kids once he read it.

Dan didn't know any of my friends in Port Washington so I thought I was pretty safe. But I always had that fear that didn't go away for many years. I was always looking over my shoulder and flinching when someone went to hug me.

In reflection, with the help of my angels and guides, it was determined that Maggie gave me the biggest gift of all—MY LIFE!

According to the guides, she was his distraction. If it had not been for her, Dan would have found me and murdered me. The guides informed Raven that Dan murdered three people and she knew that because their spirits were present. I always felt he was capable of murder and that he did indeed murder more than one person. I was not interested in speaking to them, nor was Raven. We didn't want to invite that negative energy into our space.

Prior to this knowledge it was difficult for me to forgive Maggie. Now, after learning that she gave me my life to live to have three more wonderful children and a loving relationship, I thought forgiving would be easy—at least at the moment. As time moved on, I found it difficult and my bitterness and anger remained. I thought of the satisfaction I would get if I confronted her face to face and told her that her secret is out but I realized that would be my ego talking. Maggie is not a self-aware person and she would never own any of it. My healing and forgiveness were not dependent on whether she would ever admit or own anything. So I gave up that thought, although it does creep back from time to time.

Continued to have readings:

I continue to have sessions with Raven on an as-needed basis. She's always there when I need her. My journey toward healing is never over. I am always on the path.

As time passed in North Carolina I continued to seek out various people who could continue to open me up and reach all the deep-seated stuff that was still inside of me.

It was Raven that encouraged me to do a memoir because she sees that it will help not only me but many other people. She saw me sharing with other women to help them heal.

Guides/Angels:

I went to a reader who connects people with their angels and guardians. Bringing my two granddaughters with me made it an extra special occasion. Gabby was fourteen and Cam was eight. They also got readings. The reader began by telling me my guardian is a Native American Mohawk male named Grey Eagle. He was a medicine man in his tribe and a warrior. I was a young boy in a prior life with him and he was my protector in that life. She told me he sings a healing song to me at night.

My angel's name is Daniella, and she has auburn hair, wears a shimmery gold garment, and has wings. I was told that some angels have wings and some don't. There is no difference between the two. She wanted me to know what I needed to do in this life I am doing and that I will be in this life for a long time. She also said that I am carrying many lifetimes and I need to let go of them all. It has to be about me now. It was spiritually a memorable and enlightening moment. After my reading, Gabby and Cam both had theirs done.

At the end of our beautiful readings, Cam showed us a picture she had been working on the entire time. It was a drawing of her fairy. The reader told her she has a fairy as a friend and she described her as Cam was drawing her at the same time. The image she drew was an uncanny likeness of her fairy.

That experience with my two fantastic granddaughters will always be in my heart. I think they too found it to be special. You can't always find those moments. I felt blessed.

Retrieving Lost Memories

It was apparent to me that I needed to explore my early childhood in order to realize and face the abuse and understand the negative qualities it left in me, and that were created by me, in order to survive. I still wanted to move forward and to hopefully leave the negativity behind.

I called Raven because she provides therapy to access lost memories. I set up a session with her so she could call on my guides to assist in the process of retrieving my childhood memories.

We began the session with Raven saying that Maggie and Dan both came into this life with a past in black magic. Both of their souls split during rebirth. I remember this is also what my mother told me about Maggie in another reading with another medium and it was also in the Soul Retrieval process. This was the third time I heard this, so I felt it was validated. Usually two are all the validations

I need to move forward with information from a session. This split creates a personality that is intent on bringing harm to others—in a demonic way. A psychopathic personality disorder arises from this split. Both Maggie and Dan fit this description.

Maggie was using incantations that she learned in a prior life. It was natural for her. She was a child and didn't know it was ritualistic, it just came naturally. The type of abuse that she bestowed on me came out in this session. It was difficult to hear but I could relate to it all. This is how it was described to me. My life in the crib began with my demonic sister sticking pins in my head. I was very young and still in the crib. She knew she couldn't leave any marks and risk exposing herself. So she hid the marks under my hair. This was my life in the beginning. This is the place where I learned *not to voice pain and to understand that I was alone and that no one was going to help me.* So in the crib is where the negative traits arose. This is the beginning of my journey down a path that I dreaded—down a path of negativity, control, and submissiveness and how it would manifest in my life moving forward.

My mother used to tell me how she would find me in the morning sleeping under my crib. She could never figure it out. So she started to wrap a blanket around me and pin the blanket around my body so I couldn't climb out of my crib. The pins she used were very large safety pins. They were about three to four inches long. None of that changed a thing; she continued to find me on the floor. She said the pins were removed and put into a chain in the morning. I was too young to have done that on my own. No one would have thought my sister would have been involved.

Raven had seen Maggie sticking pins in my head/hair during a meditation session. The only thing I saw was a white crib. I saw nothing else. I had not known what color my crib was prior to this. Raven saw what Maggie was doing as a ritualistic ceremony while sticking the pins in my head. Raven said it was second nature to her and she didn't even realize it, she was so young herself. She was three years older than me. That was quite a session! When I went home, it was within a few days of this session that I found a picture of me in a white crib and Maggie standing in the crib with me, bending down looking into my face and me looking back in her face. I was wearing the blanket with the large pins. Was this my validation? I believe so. I don't ever remember seeing that picture and suddenly it appeared at this moment.

Raven continued to lead me on my journey with the help of my guides. She next described an incident where Maggie would put a pillow over my face and keep it there until I was practically dead and then she would remove it. Raven said I would have to take a huge gasp of air after she removed the pillow. Her assault was always to knock the breath out of me. If I died she would be found out, so she just brought me to the brink and then allowed me to live. In my life I had a huge fear of pillows or anything else over my face. I would freak out if anyone put a pillow or covers over my face and head. This phobia points me in the direction of the origin.

Raven also saw her lay me on the floor on my stomach and strike me in the back and push me further into the floor. I have had back problems and pain for as long as I can remember and work with a massage therapist on spinal issues.

Another incident that was shown to Raven was something that I have had a partial memory of my entire life. I was about three or four years old, living in Kew Gardens, New York. I remember being in a very dark place, not sure where, with a young boy about seven or eight. I always remembered that something sexual occurred but I never thought it was bad. I thought maybe it was like "you show me yours and I'll show you mine." I never had a full memory of the incident. It traveled with me through my life but I never got weird about it. So now Raven was bringing it up. She said Maggie was there and set up the whole horrible thing. She was preparing her next vicious assault. Maggie pulled the boy's pants down, played with his penis, and told him to get on top of me. I had no underwear on, don't know why, and he got on top of me. She played this ritual three more times on different days. The validation was that I had a partial memory of this incident my whole life, but I blocked out the awful parts for self-protection.

The negative pattern created here was that "you can't trust women and men are weak." Also "not to voice pain" was reinforced here.

These patterns continued throughout my life and now in my seventies, I am finally learning to let go of what doesn't serve me anymore.

It was also revealed that Maggie continued the abuse for some time. I became her perfect victim, controlled and quiet. I became the sacrifice of her rituals.

It was also revealed that there was a possibility that Maggie and my brother, Greg, could have had a weird sexual relationship. Obviously the family incest issue has been passed down to the next generation. My brother could have been called a deviant with his sexual behavior. I remember as a child he would rub up against me when I was very young. My daughter said that she thinks he molested her on an occasion. We tried to keep her away from him but never approached him about it. How stupid we were. Young and ignorant we were and used to abuse ourselves as children. He also liked very young women/girls. I want this out in the open so it can die forever to ensure it's not carried forth to the next generation.

The guides brought Raven to the episode of Dan frying Maggie's dogs in a hot car. You see, Dan went to work and it seems their two tiny, yappy dogs got into his car and he didn't know they were there. He went to work with the dogs left in the hot car all day and when they were found they were fried dead. Those dogs were Maggie's children as much or more than her own children. Raven questioned why the guides brought up that incident and how it was connected to me. Well, it seems that Maggie put me in a hot car for a long time when I was young. Both Raven and I said at the same moment, "a blue car." My father had a blue and white Oldsmobile—blue bottom and white top. The car was in our garage because my father took the Long Island Railroad to work every day and left the car in the garage. So the access was easy for her to keep me in the car for a while. I wondered where my mother was. I wondered if this incident with the fried dogs was her payback for what she did to me in the hot car. Seems like validation.

Soul Contract Reading: 2021

A soul contract is also known as Numerology of Moses and the Spiritual Map of Life. It is based on the twenty-two characters of the Hebrew alphabet and the Star of David. It's actually the blueprint of your life hidden within your birth name, which is numerology.

The chart describes your karma and challenges, your talents, your goals and dreams and your soul destiny and life purpose.

The reading was pretty powerful and eye opening. Joseph was the reader and he told me I was an angelic presence, anointed by God. The symbol is called a YOD, which I also have in my astrology chart. This means that I came into this life already enlightened, having a higher frequency, so I didn't need to come to learn the lessons of enlightenment. My only purpose was to be of service to others. The higher frequencies are positive and loving and attract more positive emotions and the lower frequencies are ego based and can attract negativity, stress, and anxiety.

Joseph went over my beliefs that were formed due to karmic programming.

- I am separate and different from others
- I am being punished, I deserve to be punished
- I don't trust men or masculine women
- I am always disempowered by men
- My environment is hostile

Joseph said that three or more 10-1s anywhere in the chart indicates that this is the last incarnation on earth, unless I choose to be reincarnated. The 10-1 is the highest of spiritual energies, the balance of male and female energies, and an ability to relate to anyone, energies of Archangel Michael and the total belief in your God self.

I had a 10-1 in physical goals, which relates to suffering from great injustice and trauma from childhood. This manifests in difficulty in relationships.

I also had a 10-1 in physical talents, which relates to me working toward using my power properly to become a healer, teacher, and an agent of change—transforming the darkness into light.

I also had a 10-1 in soul destiny, which relates to being able to stand in this reality as the Light of God, balanced in expression and power and illuminating the pathway.

The reading revealed in a past life I failed to be an individual. There was a lack of leadership and a fear of independence. In this present life I will be drawn into situations where I will have to go it alone, assume leadership, and above all develop the courage to be myself, no matter what.

He also added that I didn't come into this life with karma because I was already enlightened. I had to create karma for myself in order for me to experience human life. Boy, I sure gave it to myself.

Needless to say, the reading blew my mind. Was he really talking about me? Joseph told me to finish my memoir because it will help a lot of people. He said I was meant to help people.

After I completed all of the different forms of therapy, I now understand some of my negative qualities and where they originated from. We all go through trauma in our lives at some point. If we can pinpoint our past and where our negative qualities reared their ugly head, maybe we can get rid of them and feel better about ourselves. We need to leave the past behind and bring awareness to our true selves. We need to communicate to our children and our grandchildren our inherited family treasures, and also the things that brought shame. The bad stuff needs to be brought out into the open and understood, so that the repressed feelings are allowed to be released. This is how future generations will heal and not continue to carry negative qualities from generation to generation.

My Sister Saved My Life!

My sister, Maggie, was three years older than I, yet our differences were more far reaching than just our ages. We were opposites in every possible way. I was the youngest sibling, so there was some jealousy as children—that's not unusual. What's unusual is that Maggie's jealousy didn't change as we came into adulthood. Instead it grew more deep-seated. It appeared my sister wanted to trade her life for mine. What was it she saw? Was it the beautiful Tudor home? Was it the fact that I didn't have to work? Could she not see past those things to realize I was married to a violent psychopath that turned my and my children's lives into a living hell?

My sister, in contrast, was married to a hardworking man who delivered bread for a living and brought his paycheck home every week. No, it wasn't glamorous, but he did the best he could. Why she thought my life married to a criminally minded husband who made big money illegally was something to envy is a mystery. Maggie was once employed as an LPN for a short time, but she never really wanted to work; instead, she wanted a husband to take care of her. It seemed as if she resented her husband for not making enough money to keep her at home. His paycheck simply wasn't sufficient to care for a family of four.

The sad part of Maggie's resentment was that I was completely unaware of it in the beginning. When I did find out, of course I asked the typical questions. Why? Could I have done anything differently? But the answers never came. I worked for years to try to understand the underlying root cause of her animosity toward me. What would cause her to be so envious that she would abuse me as an infant, and either seduce, or allow herself to be seduced, by my estranged husband, move into my house, try to replicate my life, and replace me in the eyes of my children? After years of trying to smooth out our relationship without success, I reached out to professional counselors both traditional and spiritual to find the answers I desperately needed in order to move forward with my life for my sake as well as for my family's sake. It was a tedious yet revealing process that took years to uncover and again the revelations would shake me to my core. While at this point we are estranged, at least the knowledge I gained helped me to move forward, receive closure.

During each of my different types of therapy sessions, the message was the same. "You will need to forgive your sister in order to complete your healing." But that's easier said than done.

CHAPTER 18

FINALLY LETTING GO OF BITTERNESS AND RESENTMENT

While I'm not one to hold grudges, I found it difficult to release myself from the anger over the violence and betrayal I experienced; yet I wanted desperately to move past it all. I had recovered personally, financially, and professionally; yet, I just couldn't get past the emotional baggage. Seeking professional therapists both traditional and alternative gave me the answers I needed, yet answers alone were not sufficient to alter the condition of my heart and open it up to forgiving Maggie and Dan.

One of the most difficult things to come out of my numerous therapies was the revelation that by her actions, my sister actually saved my life. How was I supposed to process this piece of information? Clearly she didn't have my interests in mind when she went about betraying me; yet the fact remains my life was saved by her actions. Was I now supposed to thank her? It was a conundrum.

I'm not going so far as to thank her, but as the experts remind me, I have to forgive her to be whole. I've since learned that forgiveness is a process. It doesn't just happen. I've come to realize that if I want to enjoy my life from here on out, I need to forgive, first and foremost for myself. How can I live an abundant life if I hold onto resentments from the past? I need it for my own peace of mind. Maggie and Dan asking me to forgive them isn't the point. They are unlikely to ever do that but I don't need them to. I will forgive them for myself. I will do it to take away the power that they will continue to exert over me if I do not forgive. I may never have a relationship with my sister, yet I can forgive her. I will do it for my husband, my children, and my grandchildren because they deserve a healthy, happy wife, mother, and grandmother.

In the end, I knew that regardless of her intention, forgiveness needed to happen. I needed it to move forward and so I did. My sister and Dan are no longer in my life and I have no feelings at all whenever their names are mentioned. Once I scaled that final hurdle and allowed myself to forgive them, I felt a huge burden lifted and a sense of relief.

Now, I no longer look over my shoulder in fear. When I think of my past trauma, I have no negative thoughts and can truthfully say I no longer respond at all. It has taken decades, but I have finally arrived at the peace I have sought for so long.

CHAPTER 19

FINAL THOUGHTS ...

Reflecting on my life and lessons learned I feel I have come into my own and that I can now move forward without the extra baggage. It's all out in the open, understood, and can be viewed and discarded. It was a heavy load to carry.

I know I have been through a lot and have brought my family along for the ride. If what I have believed my whole life is right, the kids wrote their own story and this was it. They wrote for me to be their mother; they wrote that Stan, Dan, and Tom would be their fathers and influencers in their life and that in the end they would be strong, independent, powerful, wonderful human beings because of their experiences. That's all that we can ask for. The guilt I had still resides in me but not as severe. I'm learning to move past it because it doesn't serve me.

I know now why I chose the path I did and why I made the decisions I made. Early childhood taught me not to trust, not to voice pain, to think touch was a warning that danger was imminent, to stand silent in the face of danger and fear, and that I was alone. It saddens me to think of that little girl all alone going through what she went through. I know she is still there and I want to always honor her.

I chose to get pregnant at seventeen because that's when my rebellion reared its ugly head once again. I was being abused by my sister and feeling alone and probably angry and that set me up for my poor behavior and decisions. I was conditioned to take the abuse and not speak of it—to stay silent and not utter a word.

So here comes Stan, a mean man, controlling and cold and life was what he dictated. No physical abuse but plenty of emotional and spiritual abuse. I kept quiet for a while but then one day I couldn't take any more and I left after one year.

As for Dan, I was again pregnant (rebelliousness) and feeling like I had to get married to a violent, sadistic psychopath; I kept the pattern going. Growing up with my sister primed me for someone like Dan. The devil and his disciple (Maggie) reinforced all the past behaviors (the earlier ones she helped to create when I was a child in the crib) and created new ones after her relationship with him began. The new ones I added were dishonesty, hating myself worse than before, shame, guilt, adding abortions into the mix, not being able to give my kids what they needed. My day-to-day focus was on survival; there was no time for direction and support. Going on the "Get Even Tour" was detrimental to me. I learned how to be a deceitful liar to my friends during this tour.

Now Tom was someone who really was on my side and supported me to be the best person I could be. He helped me along the way with it all. He was an active participant in our life together. Yes, we had our differences but that's normal. He is a good man with a good heart. I was never in fear of my life and neither were the kids. We were trying to be a family, whatever that was. In the beginning of our relationship, I still had those awful behaviors of staying silent and not expressing my thoughts. Others—including the kids—took it as weakness. They interpreted what they saw as Tom controlling me. Nothing could have been further from the truth. Honestly, what appeared on the surface to be Tom's control was actually me not allowing myself to grow and instead burying myself in my insecurity—Tom was merely taking up the slack. It took me a long while to overcome my fears. Going to school and working helped me to reveal my strengths and talents.

It's difficult for me to see myself as an enlightened being. I almost feel embarrassed to say it because it feels like an egotistical statement. I keep asking myself, *Who am I to give people advice on how to heal themselves? What authority do I possess?* I have seen people throughout my life calling themselves authorities when they have no life experience or credentials. I never want to be that person. For me those people operate on a lower frequency. We must never give them our power. Our power is for ourselves only.

Through a lot of soul searching and discussion with different people, I now understand that my life experiences make me an authority on the subject. I needed to go through the healing process in order to help others heal. I had to change my consciousness through healing myself and now I need to share it so I can help people find their way. I'm also here to encourage others to try new and different healing options—ones you have never tried or thought about before. I know my methods of healing are new and unusual to most people, but I'm hoping it will change your way of thinking and to try new things. I now have a new consciousness as a result of my healing journey; a consciousness that grew and overcame adversity; a consciousness that has led to self-forgiveness. Today, I see myself as a valuable person who has a lot to give, instead of the self-loathing person I was. I wish I was this person when I was bringing up my kids, at least the older three. The younger three had somewhat normal issues. They had their issues and demons but without the violence, abuse, and fear in their day-to-day living.

I would not have reached the hidden memories without the support and love of my family and my guides, past and present. Even though I have no real memory of some of my story, I have been validated enough to know that it is all real and true. Validation for me comes in various forms. The strongest one is the emotional and physical reaction I feel when I'm remembering. Why else would I have such a huge physical and emotional response when remembering the past? It means truth to me. I also rely on the people in my life that have the memory. Lying so much in my life, for whatever reason, means that now I must follow the path of truth. I have faith that the road I took for healing and forgiveness is what I signed on for in order for me to heal the karmic line. I have been told that the line is clean and I have done what I came to do. I've also been told I'm not done in this life. I still have more I need to do. I have more service to give.

I know some people think by using shamans, mediums—the "New Age Path"—is bad; that it's black magic, evil, or just fake. I am a believer in Jesus Christ. Jesus performed psychic feats, such as telepathy, reviving the dead, walking on water, psychic readings, and healings. The church calls them miracles. Why is it evil when ordinary people display these abilities? He is my savior and that's who I talk to, and I follow His teachings. The three wise men were astrologers and astronomers and followed the North Star to His manger. They were called Magi or Magicians. I don't go to church every Sunday but I don't think it's necessary in order to pray and have faith and believe. Sometimes the people that profess their religiosity are the true devils. I also believe that if you do things with evil intent, that's a reflection of the devil. Prejudice and hate are evil machinations that are devil-inspired. The term "new age" wreaks havoc with some people. New age refers to new age ideas and beliefs like reincarnation, astrology, psychics, and all things spiritual. Why is that so bad? We should allow ourselves to follow the paths that we as individuals choose to take and not to be judged because we follow a different path.

The new world of technology is going to expand us to heights never seen before. A huge change will be occurring. Our consciousness and society must change along with the changing world and we have to keep adapting to the new environment. As long as we follow some basic human principles toward each other we can thrive. We can help one another instead of hating one another. Jesus' mission was to bring spiritual salvation and eternal life to those who believe. He preached love, acceptance, compassion, forgiveness, and hope. Those are the characteristics that I want for myself, my family, and humankind.

As I write this memoir of my life, I realize I have an important message to deliver to abused and controlled women. There are so many of you out there, quietly struggling and begging silently for someone to help you escape. I know you because I've been you. As my story clearly illustrates, there isn't anyone waiting in the wings to come rescue you. Outsiders won't see the pain you live with every day. My husband controlled the finances, creating a situation where I was trapped with no place to go. I was scared to death; fear ruled my every move. I finally confided in a friend who helped me relocate after my escape, but it took ten long years to finally summon up the courage. So much physical and emotional pain and so much time lost. My story isn't an anomaly. Sadly, it's all too common. If you learn anything from my experience, it's to stop it in the beginning; be vocal, don't tolerate violent behavior, and don't allow circumstances to trap you.

Women have been fighting for equal rights forever. On March 31, 1776, Abigail Adams, wife of John Adams, the second president of the United States, was an advocate of women's rights. She opposed slavery and supported women's education. She felt that women should be part of decision making rather than just being there to serve their husbands. She said the following:

> Remember the ladies and be more generous and favorable to them than your ancestors. Do not put such unlimited power into the hands of the

husbands. Remember all men would be tyrants if they could. If particular care and attention is not paid to the ladies, we are determined to foment a rebellion, and will not hold ourselves bound by any laws in which we have no voice or representation.

In the early 1900s, women were finally granted the right to vote. Up until then women were considered second-class citizens, and unfortunately that still persists today. Before that time only white, property-owning males were allowed to vote. There were four states that allowed freed black slaves to vote but women were never allowed.

The Women's Movement of the sixties and seventies sought equal rights and opportunities and personal freedoms for women. Women weren't paid the same as men doing the same job. President Kennedy signed into law the Equal Pay Act in 1963. Today there is still inequality in pay between men and women. Up until 1974, before the help of Ruth Bader Ginsburg, women did not have the right of ownership, and were unable to get credit cards and loans without their husband's signature.

January 22, 1973 (my birthday), the Supreme Court declared that a women had the right to choose whether or not to have an abortion. Women were finally able to make their own decisions about children and families. Unfortunately, that is all at risk once more.

The "Me Too Movement" rose to the forefront around 2017, and is bringing out all the hidden evils that men have done to women to control them by either drugging them or threatening to take their livelihood away and making a mockery out of them if they don't comply with their misogynistic needs. This movement wants women to know they are not alone. Awareness is the key to stopping this epidemic so we can heal.

Women risk domestic abuse and violence, sexual harassment, dating violence, sexual assault, trafficking, etc. It's endless. When does it stop? It stops when we say no more! This is 2023 and we are still fighting for basic human rights and equality.

The white men in Congress are apathetic to women's needs. All they want to do is control our thoughts and our bodies. They want to legislate how we procreate and raise our families but they don't want to legislate to give us basic freedoms. It's time to take back the power and not hand it over to the mean, abusive people of the world who want to control us. If there is nothing else you get out of my story, please take control of your life and do what makes you happy. You can be in a relationship and still be free. Empowerment happens when you respect each other's opinions even though you don't always agree. Each individual needs to be their own true person, not who others think we should be. Together we women need to say, "NO MORE." This is my story.

AFTER HEALING: A RENEWED LIFE

Singing:

Singing has always been my passion. It began in my mother's closet and later on going to singing class with Rose and Rose teaching me how to play the guitar and sing while playing. I loved it! I was always playing music in the house and singing my favorite songs, whether I was cleaning or cooking or driving. My kids knew all the words to the music I listened to. We would all sing together.

After I retired, I volunteered to work on the Community Advisory Committee, a community group that visited nursing homes and assisted living and adult homes. I had so much experience in this area and wanted to help. I volunteered for two years and at some point became the vice chairman. It was fulfilling to a degree but after a while, I needed to do something for myself. I thought long and hard about what I wanted and needed. Singing was my answer. Early on in my retirement, I went to a singing teacher in Asheville and she taught me the rudiments of music and the mechanics of singing. I could tell she was very spiritually connected and I was in tune with that energy. One day when I went for a lesson she opened the door and said, "Today we are not singing. I got a message that you needed a healing." She laid me on the floor and went into a meditation. She told me that someone stole my voice in a prior life and she returned it to me. It blew my mind! She advised me to join a chorus. Not only would I get socially connected, I would learn about the music and get to sing.

I searched out a chorus to join and found one in Hendersonville called the Hendersonville Chorale. It is a wonderful group of people who love to sing. I met many good friends in this group. I love the experience and feel fulfilled when I sing. We have two concerts a year, one at Christmas and one in the spring. Through my participation, I have learned much about singing and reading music.

The Kids/Grandkids:

In spite of all the insanity that I have encountered on my path, I have been blessed and gifted with a wonderful family. My family is the most important thing in my life. We all worked together to do our best to hold it all together throughout some of the turmoil. We made so many mistakes but love was always there. The older three kids went through the worst and came out on the other side in great shape. My daughter Lisa says, "You can put me in the middle of a desert with nothing and I will survive." They each had their demons but have overcome the shit they had to deal with growing up.

Tee still is in contact with Stan and Margie and his brother and sister a couple of times a year. He was married and now he is divorced. He has full custody of his daughter, Gabriella, a Leo. She's Gabby or Gabalini to me. She is very smart with the capacity to accurately read people. She is into all the new age ideas, so that gives us a special bond. She seems to be heading into journalism. Tee works for a Wall Street firm and has climbed the ladder of success—all on his own without his father's help. That's key for him. He never wanted his father to say that it was because of him that Tee advanced in his career. Tee is a Gemini, which makes him playful and quick-witted. He's the jokester of the family. Geminis are fearless thinkers and social butterflies. Tee continues to have issues related to the abuse he took at the hands of Dan and also abandonment issues with his father, Stan, but he is a wonderful father and is devoted to his daughter. He is a single father raising his daughter and is doing a great job.

Lisa has no contact with her father or Maggie. At first she tried to have a relationship with the two of them but soon things changed. She began to see them for what they are and wanted no part of them. Lisa is an Aquarian and a very creative person. She has made personal training, fitness, and health her life's work. From her home she operates a gym and has clients that have been devoted to her for many years. Lisa was married twice. She has a son, Joseph, an Aries, from her first marriage. She divorced after a couple of years. Now she is married to Chris, the man who helped raise Joe and is a great father to him. Lisa and Chris are devoted to each other and to Joe. Joe is a handsome, fit, smart, savvy guy who went to Notre Dame Law School. He is now a lawyer and is married to a wonderful girl, Izzy. They now have a beautiful daughter, Lily—our first great grandchild! Lisa and Chris live part time in NY and part time in Florida. Lisa has gone through therapy and has dealt with her demons and is now focused on being healthy. She takes after my father in that way.

Kelly also has no contact with her father or Maggie. Kelly was married and has two boys, Tyler and Matthew—two incredible, handsome, loving boys. She went through a messy divorce that left her worn out. As far as the abuse she witnessed growing up, she has no memory; kind of like me, having no memories of abuse in the early years and having to go search for them—that's if you want to find them. I always tell her that even though she doesn't remember, those memories affect her. Kelly is a Leo and has that lioness outgoing personality. She is strong and can be dominating. Kelly too fought her demons and hopefully one day she'll regain some of her memories. Kelly is a successful financial advisor, and is totally independent and self-sufficient. She is vice president of her company and works with all men. She has a small stature but she is a Leo powerhouse and doesn't let anyone step on her. Tyler, a Gemini, is following in her footsteps, working with her and learning the business. He is handsome, smart, and personable. He has also finished his degree. Matt, an Aquarian, is on a path to becoming a history teacher. He is sweet and caring and absolutely gorgeous, but doesn't know it yet.

Casey is a Pisces and is a very empathetic person who is always rooting for the underdog. She is compassionate, artistic, smart, and a great teacher. Her experiences are different from her those of her older siblings. She didn't witness what the other three did. She was number four for me and one for Tom. We were in love from the second she was born, she was perfect. Lisa and Kelly and all their friends also loved her. She was like their doll and they took very good care of her. Casey is now a teacher. She has her master's degree and extra certifications and is totally independent and self-sufficient. She is not married at the moment, although she had a long-term relationship that broke up after ten years. She found out he wasn't what she thought she wanted. Casey has a lot of the same beliefs as I do, concerning breastfeeding, vaccines, and childbirth.

Seth, an Aquarian, is number five with four older siblings. Seth was a kid that had many friends and was outside playing all the time. He was very artistic from an early age. He created beautiful pictures and sculptures. After high school he went to culinary school and became a chef. He is a creative thinker, visionary, and creator of new ideas. He is now an owner of a heath food cafe in Huntington and helped create a satellite cafe in Hendersonville. His total vision is having satellite cafes and possibly food trucks to spread his healthy philosophy. He has a daughter from a prior girlfriend, Camryn, a Sagittarius. She is twelve now and is a dream and a joy to the family. I call her Cam-a-lam. Camryn and I can get into serious conversations about life. It's amazing and wonderful. Seth since has met a wonderful girl, Theresa, whom we all love. She helped him turn his life around in a wonderful way. He too had many demons he had to fight along his journey and he is now doing well. He now has something to live for—his daughter and Theresa. They moved in together and then had a wonderful son, Jesse James, a Scorpio. He is fantastic! It's terrible that we don't see him often but every chance we get we go to New York or they come here. We Facetime a lot so he can see us and remember who we are. Theresa is pregnant again and they are having a girl, so we will welcome a new grandchild into our family soon.

Ryan, a Gemini, is number six. He is the youngest of six children. Even though he is the baby, he got a lot of many different perspectives from his older siblings. He is also very creative, especially in music. He plays guitar and has written music. He is sociable and smart and very affectionate. He used to tell Tom and me that all his friends in school hated their parents. He said, "I don't hate you guys, I love you and it's so weird when they say that." Tom's mom was living with us when Ryan was born, so they became very close. Ryan loved the old people and worked with me in White Pines for eight years. He learned a lot and worked in different departments. He went to culinary school after high school. My boys like to cook, like their grandfather and mother. Ryan too had demons he needed to fight but in the end Ryan won. When we moved, he came with us to North Carolina. He became a food service manager in an assisted living facility. He ran the department like the pro he is and is now going to run the satellite Roots Cafe in Hendersonville. It's perfect for him! Ryan is a good human being and cares about humanity.

The above is a brief synopsis of my beautiful family. They are my life and I am blessed. I question a lot, why all the pregnancies and the unbelievable fertility? I don't have an answer. I can only say each one of them was meant to be in this world in this moment. I was their vehicle along with their fathers in bringing them here. The journey we all took to get here was hard but here we are. We love each other and are looking forward to what comes next.

ABOUT THE AUTHOR

Nancy is a retired director of nursing and author of *The Gravel Driveway*. She is living happy and contented in NC, with her husband Tom and pursues her creative outlets such as singing that bring her joy.

ACKNOWLEDGEMENTS

Writing your life story is very difficult and rewarding at the same time. A writing journey is not completed alone. There are many people and spirits to thank. We never journey alone, even though we feel alone sometimes. Throughout my life I have called on our Lord Jesus Christ as the one who I trust, and know He's always there for me. I thank Him every day by living a life now that he would approve of. I know my spirt guides, angels, and ancestors are always present, helping me; so I send my love to them all.

I want to give my gratitude and love to my parents for showing me unconditional love and setting up my life's foundation. I would not be the person I am today without them.

My soul was waiting for Tom to come and help me through the mess I found myself in. We were two lost souls looking for love and support. We knew from our first look that we were supposed to be together (a sign of a previous life together). Neither of us had ever experienced that before. So thank you, Tom, for finding me in that seedy bar and being my love and wall of support since we met. We love and encourage each other to be our best selves.

My children and grandchildren are the biggest blessings in my life. They inspire me to be a better person and to show them that love and family are the best feelings in the world. Each child teaches you something different about yourself. Your grandchildren teach you a truly special love without judgement. Looking at my blessings of children, now I know why I was blessed with many pregnancies. I thank them all for keeping it real.

A special shout out to Tee for naming the book. He knew the title right away and I agreed just as fast. Tee was along for the ride almost as long as I was.

Ryan created the subtitle for this book which captures the spirit and intention of my story perfectly.

My healers and therapists were the catalyst to my awareness and understanding of the large gaps of my memory loss. They were able to piece together important information that I needed to move forward. I will always be grateful for their love, support, and knowledge while on my healing journey. It was a rough road to relive some of the negativity, but it was needed and now I don't have it trapped inside of me. I am now reconditioned and have left that negativity behind and am also strong enough to walk away from toxicity rather than storm through it. So to my healers and therapists, my love for you is great and thanks just doesn't seem enough. I will pray for you always and never forget our travels through my subconscious mind in order to bring me to self-awareness.

Raven, my shaman, I will carry you in my heart for eternity. You opened me up to reorganizing my thinking about myself. I became a new person because of your guidance and your ability to see the facts that I had no memory of, or just a blurred vision of something. I'll love you forever and thank you for your love.

My love and gratitude to Flo, who was my guide through the writing process. I have never done anything like this before and Flo was there for me every step of the way. She was my editor and ghostwriter for parts of the book. We spent many days together and getting to know each other. I love her deeply because she is loving and caring, and I consider her my friend.

I must thank Joe who I met at the end of my journey. He did my Soul Contract which helped me complete my goal of writing my memoir. I was at a standstill in writing and went to him for a reading. You know how it turned out. So Joe, you are very important to me and I want to thank you for your knowledge and the positive affect you had on me. You also made me feel that my message was very important to share, which made me feel better about myself.

CPSIA information can be obtained
at www.ICGtesting.com
Printed in the USA
LVHW010502050623
748866LV00017B/895